Life-Changing Prayers

Marie D. Jones

Wallis C. Metts, Ph.D.

Gary Wilde

Publications International, Ltd.

Marie D. Jones is an ordained minister and a contributing author to numerous books, including *Echoes of Love: Sisters, Mother, Grandmother, Friends, Graduation, Wedding; Mother's Daily Prayer Book*, and *When You Lose Someone You Love: A Year of Comfort*. She is the creator/producer of Gigglebug Farms Simply Storybook Children's Videos.

Wallis C. Metts, Ph.D., chairs the department of communication at Spring Arbor University in Spring Arbor, Michigan. As a freelance writer and editor, he has been published in more than 60 periodicals and won state and national awards for news reporting and writing for children. His book credits include *Inspirations for Daily Living, Promises of the Bible, Daily Prayer Book: Prayers for Our Country*, and *Children's Book of the Bible*.

Gary Wilde is an author who has written numerous educational and devotional magazine articles and books, including *Bedside Book of Prayers, The Promise of Faith, Simple Prayers and Blessing*, and *God's Daily Inspirations*. One of his ongoing projects is editing the devotional quarterly, *Quiet Hour*.

ACKNOWLEDGMENTS:

Page 10: Excerpt from *My Life in Christ* by St. John of Kronstadt, published by Holy Trinity Monastery Press, Jordanville, NY 13361. Reprinted by permission of Holy Trinity Monastery.

Page 13: Excerpt from *Yet Will I Trust Him* by Peg Rankin. Copyright © 1980. Reprinted by permission of Gospel Light/Regal Books, Ventura, CA 93003.

Pages 28, 180, 204–205: Excerpts from *Adventures in Prayer* by Catherine Marshall. Copyright © 1975 by Catherine Marshall. Copyright © 2001 by Marshall-LeSourd L.L.C. Used with permission. All rights reserved. Find other titles by best-selling inspirational author Catherine Marshall at your favorite bookstore, including *Christy, Beyond Our Selves, The Helper,* and *Moments that Matter*. Visit www.CatherineMarshall.com for more information.

Pages 31, 45: Excerpts from *The Prayers of Peter Marshall* edited by Catherine Marshall. Copyright © 1954. Reprinted by permission of Chosen Books, Inc., a division of Baker Book House Company.

Page 52: Excerpt from "Take My Hand, Precious Lord" by Thomas Dorsey. Copyright © 1932. Reprinted by permission of Warner/Chappell Music, Inc.

Page 56: Excerpt from *31 Days of Praise* by Ruth Myers. Copyright © 1994 by Warren and Ruth Myers. Reprinted by permission of Multnomah Publishers Inc.

Page 62: Excerpts from "The Road Ahead" from *Thoughts in Solitude* by Thomas Merton. Copyright © 1958 by the Abbey of Our Lady of Gethsemani. Copyright renewed 1986 by the Trustees of the Thomas Merton Legacy Trust. Reprinted by permission of Farrar, Straus and Giroux, LLC.

Page 82: Excerpt from "To God for Guidance" from *The Prayers of Pope John Paul II* edited by Paul Thigpen, published by Servant Publications. Copyright © 1996.

Pages 84, 316: Excerpts from *Silence of the Heart: Meditations by Mother Teresa of Calcutta* compiled by Kathryn Spink. Copyright © 1985. Reprinted by permission of SPCK.

Page 118: Excerpt from "God of Grace and God of Glory" by Harry Emerson Fosdick. Copyright © 1954. Reprinted by permission of Brodt Music Company, Inc.

Page 122: Excerpt from *The Practice of the Presence of God with Spiritual Maxims* by Brother Lawrence. Copyright © 1958, 1967 by Fleming H. Revell, a division of Baker Book House Company.

Page 126: Excerpt from "Beneath the Cross of Christ" from *The Prayers of Pope John Paul II* edited by Paul Thigpen, published by Servant Publications. Copyright © 1996.

Page 153: Excerpt from *Treasury of Comfort* edited by Sidney Greenberg. Copyright © 1954 by Crown Publishers, Inc., New York, NY. Reprinted by permission of the American Foundation for the Blind, Helen Keller Archives.

Page 155: Excerpt from *All the Days* by Vance Havner. Copyright © 1976. Reprinted by permission of Fleming H. Revell, a division of Baker Book House Company.

Page 199: Excerpt from *More Precious than Silver* by Joni Eareckson Tada. Copyright © 1998 by Joni Eareckson Tada. Reprinted by permission of Zondervan.

Page 225: Excerpt from "Sunday School Prayers" in *The Negro's Church* by Benjamin Elijah Mays and Joseph William Nicholson. Copyright © 1933. Reprint 1969 by Arno Press, NY. Reprinted by permission of Bernice Mays Perkins of the former Mays Estate, niece and co-executor of the former Mays Estate.

Page 245: "Serenity" by Reinhold Niebuhr. Reprinted by permission of the estate of Reinhold Niebuhr.

Page 269: Excerpt from *Contemporary Prayers for Public Worship* edited by Caryl Micklem. Copyright © 1967. Reprinted by permission of SCM Press.

Page 272: Excerpt from *Toward Jerusalem* by Amy Carmichael. Copyright © 1989. Reprinted by permission of SPCK.

Pages 278, 279: Excerpts from *Alcoholics Anonymous*. The excerpts from the book *Alcoholic Anonymous* are reprinted with permission of Alcoholics Anonymous World Services, Inc. (AAWS). Permission to reprint these excerpts does not mean that A.A.W.S. has reviewed or approved the contents of this publication, or that A.A.W.S. necessarily agrees with the views expressed herein. A.A. is a program of recovery from alcoholism *only* – use of these excerpts in connection with programs and activities that are patterned after A.A., but which address other problems, or in any other non A.A. context, does not imply otherwise. Additionally, while A.A. is a spiritual program, A.A. is not a religious program. Thus, A.A. is not affiliated or allied with any sect, denomination, or specific religious belief.

Page 290: Excerpt from *The Quiet Answer* by Hugh Prather. Copyright © 1991. Reprinted by permission of Hugh Prather, author of *Love and Courage* (Conari Press).

Pages 314–315: Excerpt from *God's Missionary* by Amy Carmichael. Reprinted by permission of CLC Publications, Fort Washington, PA.

Scripture quotations marked NIV are taken from *The Holy Bible, New International Version*. Copyright © 1973, 1978, 1984, International Bible Society. Used by permission of Zondervan Publishing House. All rights reserved.

Scripture quotations marked NKJV are taken from the *New King James Version*. Copyright © 1979, 1980, 1982 by Thomas Nelson, Inc. Used by permission. All rights reserved.

Scripture taken from the *New Revised Standard Version* of the Bible. Copyright © 1989 by the Division of Christian Education of the National Council of the Churches of Christ in the USA. Used by permission. All rights reserved.

 Contents

Praying to a Life-Changing God

Through the ages, people have considered prayer to be one of life's greatest blessings. Prayer, for them, is often life changing. Within these pages you'll discover heartfelt prayers that invite you to slow down, take a few moments of "time out" in your day, and consider the life-changing God who loves you. What you do with these prayers—your thoughts about them and your ways of applying their power—could open new vistas along your spiritual journey.

Change often begins with a simple act of receiving. Our hope is that the prayers and insights about the prayers in this book will be, for you, a gift from the hand of God. After all, our prayers are ultimately motivated by the one to whom we pray, the one who gives us the ability to utter words of praise, thanks, petition, or lament.

You'll find all of these sentiments in the prayers in this book. Meanwhile, you may wish to spend a few moments each day with them, reading through a prayer during a quiet time. At other times, you'll desire a longer session, letting several prayers warm your heart and define your vision. In either case, remember that prayer is both an *action* and an *attitude*. We pray whenever we create space in our day to become aware of God's presence. We pray with words, but we can also pray without words. For God not only hears our minds, but he also observes our hearts.

This book includes many of the best-known and often-repeated prayers. Read and consider them anew so that they might open your mind to new thoughts about God. May they also speak gently to your heart about life-changing ways to move ahead along the pathways of the Spirit. For spiritual growth is truly a step-by-step process. It evolves each day, with each decision to place our lives once again into the hands of God.

Learning to Pray

O God,
Early in the morning I cry unto You.
Help me to pray
And to think only of You.

Dietrich Bonhoeffer

Jesus Loves Me

Jesus loves me! This I know,
for the Bible tells me so.
Little ones to him belong;
they are weak, but he is strong.
Yes, Jesus loves me! Yes, Jesus loves me!
Yes, Jesus loves me! The Bible tells me so.

Anna B. Warner

When Anna B. Warner wrote this renowned hymn in 1860, it was part of a poem that appeared in a novel co-written with Anna's sister, Susan. It wasn't long before this profound yet simple declaration of Jesus' love for his children became a universally known and loved prayerlike hymn all across the globe, sung by millions of children and adults in dozens of languages.

For many of us, this hymn was the first one we learned to speak or sing in church or Sunday school. It served to introduce us to God's promise of love, as told in the Bible through his Son, Jesus. With a child's innocence and purity of faith, the words speak to us of a truth that cannot be disputed—that we are all to come to Jesus for relationship and we will forever be loved and cared for by him. After all, the Bible tells us so.

Especially powerful is the line "they are weak, but he is strong," for this means that we have a champion in heaven, a loving Creator who cares not if we are weak or scared or small in stature. Jesus stated we must become "like children" if we are to enter the kingdom of God, and this sweet, simple hymn reminds us all, no matter our age, of this wonderful truth.

God chose what is weak in the world to shame the strong.

1 Corinthians 1:27

The Mind of a Child

At that time Jesus said, "I thank you, Father, Lord of heaven and earth, because you have hidden these things from the wise and the intelligent and have revealed them to infants; yes, Father, for such was your gracious will."

Matthew 11:25–26

In this simple prayer, Jesus was making it quite clear that anyone can grasp God's truths conveyed in the gospel message. You don't have to be especially intelligent or educated to understand. In fact, you need have only an open mind like a child's.

There is nothing wrong with wisdom and being smart, but when it comes to connecting with God, children know something most adults have forgotten—that the analytical mind has nothing to do with it. Knowing and loving God is the realm of the heart in its most childlike state of awe and faith.

Lord, grant me a simple, kind, open, believing, loving and generous heart, worthy of being your dwelling place.

John Sergieff

Bonhoeffer's Last Prayer

O God,
Early in the morning I cry unto You.
Help me to pray
And to think only of You.
I cannot pray alone.
In me there is darkness
But with You there is light.

Dietrich Bonhoeffer

A man of many accomplishments, Dietrich Bonhoeffer was a lifelong student of religion and eventually was ordained as a pastor in the German Evangelical Church. He was a highly influential scholar and leader during the 1930s, but his greatest challenge came in the spring of 1943 when, as the leader of the anti-Nazi Confessing Church, he was captured and imprisoned in a Nazi concentration camp for trying to help Jews escape to Switzerland.

Bonhoeffer wrote this prayer for his fellow concentration camp prisoners before being hung at Flossenburg

We are so limited in our perspective, God. We know you see things from an eternal viewpoint and that you ask us to trust that you are wise and loving. But when everything around us and within us seems to cry out that you are unjust, please hold steady our faith in your unfailing goodness.

on April 9, 1945. His words live on today as a reminder that no matter where we are in life, God is there, and that no matter how dark things appear to be, God can be the light we seek. If a man in Bonhoeffer's terrible position could find a reason not to turn his back on God but continue to praise and trust God, surely we can, too.

In this powerful prayer of petition, thanksgiving, and surrender, the words speak of a man struggling to overcome the darkness within, as well as the fear, anger, and restlessness that weaken the mind and spirit. And considering his position, who could blame him for his bitterness? But his prayer tells us

Sometimes when reading accounts of innocent prisoners facing death, I become impressed with the intensity of life that they seem to be experiencing. The importance of every moment is heightened as death awaits its prey. In a strange way I feel left out; it's not that I covet their pain. But I do become aware that I am reading stories of individuals who are experiencing a fullness of life that very few people know.

Peg Rankin,
Yet Will I Trust Him

that with God we can find the antidote to that same fear, anger, and restlessness. With God we can find light, peace, comfort, companionship, and patience.

Bonhoeffer must have known the terrible fate that awaited him, for he later states he was ready to accept tribulation from God's hand, knowing that he would not be given more to deal with than he could bear. If we remember this when our own trials challenge us, we can overcome even the greatest obstacles in our path, for truly, as the last line reads, God does make all things work together for the good of his children.

We may not understand how or why God works in the ways he does, but we have faith in him all the same.

Dietrich Bonhoeffer was born in Breslau, Germany. He became a student at the University of Berlin and was awarded his doctorate with honors in 1927, later becoming an important part of the European ecumenical movement. He assumed a post as lecturer at the University of Berlin, and he also served as curate for a German church in Spain before becoming a pastor and eventual leader of the Confessing Church in Germany. His spiritual life flourished, as did his life as a writer, musician, and author of poetry. He was one of four immediate family members to die at the hands of the Nazi regime for participating in the Protestant resistance. To this day, he is considered one of the most important theologians of the twentieth century.

Forgive Me, Lord

O My God, I am heartily sorry for having offended Thee. I detest all my sins, because I dread the loss of Heaven, and the pains of Hell. But most of all, because they offend Thee My God, Who art all good, and deserving of all my love. And I firmly resolve, with the help of Thy grace, to confess my sins, to do penance, and to amend my life.

Act of Contrition

Millions of people have spoken this prayer as part of their confession, asking God to forgive them for their sins and offenses. As we grow in our faith in Christ, we continue to fall short of the mark. Therefore, we repeat this reverent prayer to God, offering repentance and pleading for grace.

We detest it when we sin, but because we have human weaknesses, we fail now and then. Therefore, we must look to God for the promise of heaven that awaits those who come before him

and ask for forgiveness. This requires humility, honesty, and the courage to take responsibility for our mistakes.

No matter how old we are, we sin. When we do, we know that we can go before God as humble servants ready and willing to make amends and do what is necessary to walk once again in his light. With a firm resolve, we vow to do better each day as we mature as Christians.

Prayer can bring us back into a relationship with God if we've been straying. Confession is a key element of our prayers. Moreover, forgiven people forgive others. As we seek peace with God, God may urge us to seek peace with someone else.

The Lord's Prayer

Our Father in heaven, hallowed be your name. Your kingdom come. Your will be done, on earth as it is in heaven. Give us this day our daily bread. And forgive us our debts, as we also have forgiven our debtors. And do not bring us to the time of trial, but rescue us from the evil one.

Matthew 6:9–13

In a conversation with his disciples, Jesus was asked how they should pray. Jesus' answer to their question is known as "The Lord's Prayer." Jesus told them not to "heap up empty phrases . . . for your Father knows what you need before you ask him" (Matt. 6:7–8). Nor should they pray in order to be seen praying, but they should "go into [their] room and shut the door and pray to [their] Father who is in secret; and [their] Father who sees in secret will reward [them]" (Matt. 6:6).

Jesus knew that praying publicly in order to receive the attention of others does not please God but that praying privately is what impresses God. He also pointed out that for prayer to be effective a person should pray in a place where the person can be in quiet meditation, whether that place is a silent room or the serenity of the inner soul.

Most important to Jesus was that a person should not ask for something without first offering praise and thanksgiving to God. "The Lord's Prayer" begins with the lines "Our Father in heaven, hallowed be your name. Your kingdom come. Your will be done, on earth as it is in heaven."

Jesus taught his disciples to pray: "Forgive us our debts, as we also have forgiven our debtors." Ultimately, he modeled forgiveness when he prayed on the cross: "Father, forgive them; for they do not know what they are doing." We are not to forgive only when it is convenient for us. Forgiveness is meant not just for those who hurt us unintentionally, but for anyone who has temporarily strayed from the path.

We begin with these words of praise and honor for God's mighty power and glory in his holy name. We want God to know how much we love him and how grateful we are for his blessings. We also want God to know that his will is more important than our own and that we will do what he instructs us to do. In other words, we let God know that we are willing to be changed and moved by him.

In the lines that follow, Jesus instructed the disciples to make their petition known to God: "Give us this day our daily bread. And forgive us our debts, as we also have forgiven our debtors. And do not bring us to the time of trial, but rescue us

from the evil one." These words let God know that we desire sustenance from him, his forgiveness for our sins, and his protection from tribulations and evil.

There is a catch, however, for in order to receive forgiveness for our "debts," whether they are financial, emotional, or spiritual, we must *also* forgive our "debtors"—those who have sinned against us. Jesus emphasized the power and importance of forgiveness when he said, "For if you forgive others their trespasses, your heavenly Father will also forgive you; but if you do not forgive others, neither will your Father forgive your trespasses" (Matt. 6:14–15).

When we pray "The Lord's Prayer," we enter into a covenant with God, a promise to be merciful to others and receive God's blessings in return. For if we are able to open our hearts and forgive those who have harmed us, we will be blessed with God's forgiveness as well. Not only do we receive the gift of a clean slate with others, but we also experience the prosperity of God's sustenance—"our daily bread"—each and every day.

What makes this particular prayer so wonderful and life changing is that the words came out of Jesus' own mouth as the perfect way for us to pray. "The Lord's Prayer" contains all the elements of a simple yet powerful prayer that is guaranteed to be answered by God. Perhaps this is why "The Lord's Prayer" has become the most often-repeated, best-loved of all Christian prayers.

What Prayer Is—and Isn't

*Your method of prayer isn't nearly as important as what you're
trying to accomplish when you pray. We need to understand
what prayer is and what it isn't.*

*For one thing, prayer is not manipulation. We don't force God to do
things by praying often, loudly, or with some secret formula. Jesus
made a point of criticizing those who made a big show of their prayers
"on the street corners."*

*Instead, Jesus said, you should "go into your room and shut the door"
and then pray. Some people have literally created a prayer closet
where they withdraw from the world to spend time with God. That's
nice but not necessary. Jesus was saying prayer is a private
conversation between you and the Lord. Just talk with God.*

The Gift of Hardship

Lord, make possible for me by grace what is impossible to me by nature. You know that I am not able to endure very much, and that I am downcast by the slightest difficulty.

Grant that for Your sake I may come to love and desire any hardship that puts me to the test, for salvation is brought to my soul when I undergo suffering and trouble for You.

Thomas á Kempis

My brothers and sisters, whenever you face trials of any kind, consider it nothing but joy.

James 1:2

Down through the ages the saints have learned to thank God for their troubles, confident that he will use their troubles to make them—and the world—better.

It's not easy to "love and desire" hardship, as this prayer suggests, but it is a mark of maturity to see its significance, welcoming it as an opportunity to trust God and see him work.

Learning to pray this way always draws us closer to the God we love and in whom we place our trust.

A Night of Prayer

Because your steadfast love is better than life, my lips will praise you. So I will bless you as long as I live; I will lift up my hands and call on your name. My soul is satisfied as with a rich feast, and my mouth praises you with joyful lips when I think of you on my bed, and meditate on you in the watches of the night; for you have been my help, and in the shadow of your wings I sing for joy. My soul clings to you; your right hand upholds me.

Psalm 63:3–8

During his last year in college, my son Christian, a graphic artist, developed the habit of working all night in his studio, especially as he prepared for his senior honors show. Unfortunately, he would often fall asleep and miss classes. We joked with him, calling him nocturnal and pointing out that the world actually operated on a different schedule.

Actually, Christian had to work at night, which became the only time he could really focus on his work. Because he is very good at what he does, many demands were on his time and talent. In fact, I've seen him make hundreds of dollars in a single hour!

Sometimes prayer is like that. Night is the only time we have to focus on God and his grace. Our days are so filled with decisions and responsibilities that it is very late when we find the time to converse with God.

According to the Gospel of Luke, Jesus himself spent the entire night in prayer before he called and named his apostles. In doing this, Jesus was like many others who have sought God's wise counsel late at night.

Like the writer of this prayer, late at night we finally meditate on God. Free from other distractions, we discover fresher insights and greater joy. These late night prayers can be rewarding, even deliriously so. We are "satisfied as with a rich feast."

When we've done this often enough, we have something to hang in the gallery of our lives, a portrait of grace created "under the shadow of his wings."

bide with me; fast falls the eventide;
The darkness deepens; Lord, with me abide!
When other helpers fail, and comforts flee,
Help of the helpless, O abide with me.
Swift to its close ebbs out life's little day;
Earth's joys grow dim, its glories pass away.
Change and decay in all around I see;
O thou who changest not, abide with me.

Henry Lyte, "Abide With Me"

Be Patient

Lord Jesus, you know how long I have been praying about this, and I have tried to be patient about an answer. But Lord, why does your providence have to move so slowly?

I know the seasons come and go in majestic sequence. The earth rotates on its axis in a predetermined rhythm. No prayers of mine can change any of this.

But how do I, so earth bound, come to terms with the pace of eternity?

I want to be teachable, Lord. Is there something you want to show me, some block you want removed, some change in me or my attitude before you can answer my prayer? Give me the gift of eyes that see, of ears that hear what you are saying to me.

Catherine Marshall, *Adventures in Prayer*

God always answers prayer but not always with the answer we want. Sometimes it is "Yes." Sometimes it is "No." And sometimes it is "Wait."

"Wait" is the hardest answer of all, but it is one designed right into the universe. Like the farmer who waits for rain, we have to wait for the answer to our prayers. Everything runs on God's schedule, not ours.

It is while we wait that we are transformed. The seed draws nourishment from the deep, dark soil, just as the Spirit of God enriches us with insight and virtue, feeding us with his grace. During this time we learn to trust him and listen to him. We learn what Catherine Marshall here calls "the pace of eternity."

And it all happens while we wait and pray.

See how the farmer waits for the land to yield its valuable crop and how patient he is for the autumn and spring rains. You too, be patient and stand firm, because the Lord's coming is near.

James 5:7–8 NIV

The Lord's Own Way

Have thine own way, Lord! Have thine own way!
Thou art the potter, I am the clay.
Mold me and make me after thy will,
While I am waiting, yielded and still.

Have thine own way, Lord! Have thine own way!
Search me and try me, Savior today!
Wash me just now, Lord, wash me just now,
as in thy presence I humbly bow.

Have thine own way, Lord! Have thine own way!
Wounded and weary, help me I pray!
Power, all power, surely is thine!
Touch me and heal me, Savior divine!

Have thine own way, Lord! Have thine own way!
Hold o'er my being absolute sway.
Fill with thy Spirit till all shall see
Christ only, always, living in me!

Adelaide Addison Pollard

The power of surrendering to God's will for our lives is evident in this hymn by Adelaide Addison Pollard. Written in 1907, Pollard was struggling with her desire to become a missionary in Africa, but her attempts to raise necessary funds proved unsuccessful. She attended a prayer meeting and heard another woman surrendering her life to God. Encouraged, Pollard went home and wrote these words: "Have thine own way, Lord!"

Pollard understands that we should live not by our will but God's will, for God knows best what we need. Often, we struggle on a path we think is right for us only to have our lives take a mysterious detour that leads us into new opportunities and experiences. Is it the hand of God pushing us onto a side road we had never considered?

If we are struggling with a sense of frustration and discouragement, it is

We remember all too well the bitter discoveries we have made when we have tried to run our lives our own way, when we try to steer our own craft. Wilt Thou come aboard, Lord Jesus, and set us on a true course?

Peter Marshall

because we have tried to take control and "make things happen." Instead, we should listen to the guidance of our inner voice and let life unfold naturally. By forcing life to look a certain way, usually based upon past illusions, we miss out on the life of purpose and fulfillment God intended for us.

When we allow ourselves to be like clay in the potter's hands, as Pollard writes, we find we are molded into something far greater than we had ever envisioned. When we allow God to guide and direct our paths, we discover a life we never imagined possible in our limited thinking. By surrendering to the divine flow of God's love expressed through us, we will experience blessings in abundance. Life will no longer be a struggle. We will no longer be stuck in a rut of our own making.

"Mold me and make me after Thy will," Pollard asked willingly in her hymn of faithful surrender all those years ago. God did answer her, for she not only went on to Africa and

Scotland as a missionary but also became a teacher and the author of more than 100 hymns and Gospel songs.

What miracles can surrendering to God's will bring to your life?

Lift up Your Heart

Lift up your heart in sweet surrender to the God who is waiting to shower you with blessings. Lift up your soul on wings of joy to the God who is waiting to guide you from the chaos and shadows out into the light of a peace that knows no equal.

A Prayerful Journey

The Lord is your keeper; the Lord is your shade at your right hand. The sun shall not strike you by day, nor the moon by night.

The Lord will keep you from all evil; he will keep your life. The Lord will keep your going out and your coming in from this time on and forevermore.

Psalm 121:5–8

Now I lay me down to sleep,
I pray the Lord my soul to keep;
If I should die before I wake,
I pray the Lord my soul to take.

Unknown

This ancient Hebrew prayer of pilgrimage is about the specific fears of travelers. Saying this prayer as a protective cover, they believed the Lord would keep them from sunstroke on the hot dusty roads and from being moonstruck, which they thought caused insanity. Despite their superstition, this prayer can be appropriate for us, for it rightfully assumes an excellent promise: Truly the Lord will keep us.

Newton's Amazing Grace

Amazing Grace! How sweet the sound,
That saved a wretch like me!
I once was lost, but now am found,
Was blind, but now I see.

Twas grace that taught my heart to fear,
And grace my fears relieved.
How precious did that grace appear
The hour I first believed.

Thro' many dangers, toils and snares,
I have already come;
Tis grace hath bro't me safe thus far,
And grace will lead me home.

When we've been there ten thousand years,
Bright shining as the sun,
We've no less days to sing God's praise
Than when we first begun.

John Newton

If anyone could have proclaimed the power of God's merciful grace, it was John Newton. At age 7, he lost his mother, and by age 11, he hit the high seas with his father. Soon he became a man of reckless abandon and godlessness, serving on ships that enslaved people in Africa and sold them to visiting slave traders. Eventually Newton became captain of his own slave ship, but his wicked life would be challenged when he encountered a violent storm at sea that would change his life and inspire him to write this classic hymn.

During that storm, Newton read Thomas à Kempis's book, *Imitation of Christ,* and the book's message, com-

bined with the frightening storm, served as the basis for Newton's eventual acceptance of Christ as his Savior. Thus began a spiritual journey that over the years would transform him from a wretched sinner to a crusader for Christ's teachings. At the age of 39, he was ordained an Anglican minister. He died at age 82, a man of great faith and gratitude for God's grace, which he believed had saved his soul.

"Amazing Grace" has gone on to become one of the greatest, most repeated hymns of all time, sung across the world in churches and centers of worship and at funerals and military memorials. A variety of musical artists have performed it in every style. But to those of us who feel a personal call to this prayerful hymn, its words describe our own quiet and reverent awe of a god who could save even the most lowly and sinful and restore spiritual vision to those blinded by fear.

That something as mysterious as grace exists for all of us—no matter how poor, lost, or distraught—gave Newton reason to sing out in praise of God. He wanted to thank God for watching over him even in his darkest and most troubled moments, times he described as "many dangers, toils and snares." Even now, millions of people the world over have experienced that very grace in their own lives. They have felt their hearts soar in joyful praise for the goodness of a God who never deserts us.

Whether we whisper, speak, shout, or sing "Amazing Grace" matters not, for the words harbor such transforming power and humility in any form, especially when we are at a place in our lives when we are ready and willing to give our-

selves to God. That is what makes this prayer so profound. It speaks of despair, hope, renewal, and salvation.

That a wretch could be saved, that those of us who feel lost, alone, and afraid could be led home again, that we are safe in God's eternal love no matter how we've sinned or what mistakes we've made—these are the wonderful messages of "Amazing Grace."

How sweet it is!

Amazing Gains

Just when all seems hopeless, prayer lifts us like a wave on the ocean. Prayer doesn't hide from pain but uses it like the force of the sea to move us to a new place of insight, patience, courage, and sympathy. Always, it is God's hand beneath the surface holding us up.

Isaiah's Request

O Lord, be gracious to us; we wait for you. Be our arm every morning, our salvation in the time of trouble.

Isaiah 33:2

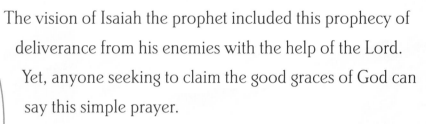

The vision of Isaiah the prophet included this prophecy of deliverance from his enemies with the help of the Lord. Yet, anyone seeking to claim the good graces of God can say this simple prayer.

By waiting on the Lord, we are rewarded with the salvation we need and the shield we desire from our own enemies, whether they be physical or mental in nature. Like a protective arm, God's might wraps around us, sheltering us in times of trouble.

In the arena of adversity, the Scriptures teach us three essential truths:
God is completely sovereign.
God is infinite in wisdom.
God is perfect in love.

Jerry Bridges, *Trusting God—Even When Life Hurts*

The Sign of the Cross

In the name of the Father, and of the Son, and of the Holy Spirit, amen.

The words to "The Sign of the Cross" are second nature to Catholics throughout the world. At an early age, children in the Catholic Church learn to place their left hand on their chest and move their right hand to their forehead as they say,

When a priest is about to read the Gospel at Mass, he makes "The Sign of the Cross" on his forehead, lips, and chest. The sign on the forehead indicates his belief in the Good News of Christ's Gospel. The sign on the lips enjoins him to preach the word of the Gospel by mouth. The sign on the chest indicates that he treasures the presence of the Lord and his words deep within his heart.

"In the name of the Father," then move their right hand to their chest as they say, "and the Son," and then touch their right hand to their left shoulder and across to their right shoulders as they say, "and of the Holy Spirit, amen."

This simple gesture, spoken and acted out at the beginning and ending of prayers, symbolizes many things to Christians. It represents the cross at Calvary, where Jesus was crucified. It represents the triune nature of God as the Father, Son, and Holy Ghost. It represents belief in Christ and his embodiment of both the human and the divine.

When we make "The Sign of the Cross," we are inviting God's presence into our lives, almost as if we are opening a door through which the Spirit of the Lord can enter and be with us. Whether we are praying when a priest is blessing someone during the Mass, or in times of fear and temptation, or as a demonstration of belief, "The

Sign of the Cross" brings us closer to God and his comfort, love, and strength.

"The Sign of the Cross" and its accompanying prayer are reverent displays of our faith and trust in the Lord. They serve to remind us of Jesus' ultimate sacrifice for our sins, and they are our shield against all that is evil. They protect us, unite us, and empower us. They are a daily expression of our relationship with God.

If on our daily course our mind
Be set to hallow all we find,
New treasures still of countless price
God will provide for sacrifice.
The trivial round, the common task
Will furnish all we ought to ask;
Room to deny ourselves—a road
To bring us daily nearer God.

John Keble

The Singing Fire

You keep my eyelids from closing; I am so troubled that I cannot speak. I consider the days of old, and remember the years of long ago. I commune with my heart in the night; I meditate and search my spirit: "Will the Lord spurn forever, and never again be favorable? Has his steadfast love ceased forever? Are his promises at an end for all time? Has God forgotten to be gracious? Has he in anger shut up his compassion?"

Psalm 77:4–9

Susannah Spurgeon, wife of a famous English preacher, was bedridden for 15 years. One night, after a particularly long and restless day, she says the darkness entered her very soul, and she prayed, asking God, "Why do you permit lingering weakness to hinder the sweet service I long to render to your poor servants?"

There was no answer, and the only sound she heard was the crackling of an oak log in the fireplace. Suddenly, however, she heard a clear musical note, like the trill of a robin, and wondered where it was coming from, considering both the time of year and the time of day.

Eventually Susannah realized what was causing the sound. In her words, "The fire was letting loose the imprisoned music from the old oak's innermost heart!" This event deeply moved her. Later, she wrote that "when the fire of affliction draws songs of praise from us, then indeed we are purified, and our God is glorified."

Like the psalmist, she spent many nights praying and weeping and searching. And like the psalmist she at last found

Let me meditate upon the dark nights through which I have come, the sinister things from which I have been delivered— and have a grateful heart.

Peter Marshall, *The Prayers of Peter Marshall*

both strength and joy in God's revelation of himself, which often comes only in our darkest hours.

St. John of the Cross, while imprisoned for his faith, called this the "dark night of the soul," and he said it was not only likely but also necessary if we are to grow deeper in our spiritual life.

Only then, like Susannah, will we hear singing in the fire.

Love is too often like a glow-worm, showing but little light except it be in the midst of surrounding darkness. Hope itself is like a star— not to be seen in the sunshine of prosperity, and only to be discovered in the night of adversity.

Charles Spurgeon

Even the darkness will not be dark to you; the night will shine like the day, for darkness is as light to you.

Psalm 139:12 NIV

Be Alert and Pray

Jesus came out and went, as was his custom, to the Mount of Olives; and the disciples followed him. When he reached the place, he said to them, "Pray that you may not come into the time of trial." Then he withdrew from them about a stone's throw, knelt down, and prayed, "Father, if you are willing, remove this cup from me; yet, not my will but yours be done."

Then an angel from heaven appeared to him and gave him strength. In his anguish he prayed more earnestly, and his sweat became like great drops of blood falling down on the ground.

When he got up from prayer, he came to the disciples and found them sleeping because of grief, and he said to them, "Why are you sleeping? Get up and pray that you may not come into the time of trial."

Luke 22:39–46

I would like to be able to pray as Jesus did on the Mount of Olives with so much passion that the ground would be wet with my bloodlike sweat. I would also like to pray as earnestly for the same thing—that the Father's will would be done. The truth is, in learning how to pray, I have to start with the same problem the disciples had: How to stay awake. Why is it that when we should be praying, we are often sleeping? The eyes close, the head nods, and we find ourselves falling asleep in the soft, comfortable warmth of our bed.

The disciples had been through a hard, busy week. I'm sure they had good intentions, but when they reclined on the

grass in the Garden of Gethsemane, they went right to sleep. So the second time Jesus asked them to pray, he told them to "get up," for he knew what was about to occur.

The real reason they couldn't stay awake was because they didn't know what was going to happen. If they had known a band of soldiers was coming to take Jesus prisoner, they would have been wide awake, calling on God for help. They just didn't know what was going to happen next.

Neither do we. That's a good reason for us to be awake and diligent when we pray. Jesus said, "Get up and pray that you may not come into the time of trial." These are wise words to heed.

I lift up my eyes to the hills—from where does my help come? My help comes from the Lord, who made heaven and earth. He will not let your foot be moved; he who keeps you will not slumber. He who keeps Israel will neither slumber nor sleep.

Psalm 121:1–4

Following God's Will

Heavenly Father, in you we live and move and have our being: We humbly pray you will guide and govern us by your Holy Spirit.

Book of Common Prayer

Precious Lord

Precious Lord, take my hand,
Lead me on, let me stand,
I am tired, I am weak, I am worn;
Thru the storm, thru the night,
Lead me on to the light,
Take my hand, precious Lord,
Lead me home.

When the darkness appears and the night draws near,
And the day is past and gone,
At the river I stand,
Guide my feet, hold my hand;
Take my hand, precious Lord,
Lead me home.

Thomas Andrew Dorsey, "Precious Lord, Take My Hand"

Thomas Dorsey started his career playing backup for famous blues singers. Then, in the 1920s, he began to write songs about faith. A self-taught pianist, his interests switched back and forth from bawdy blues lyrics to church choral music until

1932 when his wife Nettie died in childbirth. To console himself he wrote this famous prayer song, "Precious Lord,
Take My Hand."

From then on, he never turned back from writing Christian music. He eventually became known as the "Father of
Gospel Music." In fact, he coined the term "gospel music"
for songs of worship with the bounce and rhythm of
early blues and jazz. Eventually, he composed over
1,000 gospel songs before his death in 1991. One
of those songs was "Peace in the Valley," which
both Elvis Presley and Red Foley turned into
gold records.

"Precious Lord, Take My Hand" turned out
to be the most famous of his hymns. It has encouraged millions to find comfort in the Lord's guidance
and care. As only he can, the Lord used Dorsey's dark time
to lead others to the light.

*For I am the Lord, your God, who takes hold of your right hand and
says to you, Do not fear; I will help you.*

Isaiah 41:13 NIV

What God Wants

He said, "Abba, Father, for you all things are possible; remove this cup from me; yet, not what I want, but what you want."

Mark 14:36

In the garden of Gethsemane, Jesus felt the fear of impending doom coming down upon him. He knew he would be

betrayed. He knew he would be arrested. He knew he would be crucified. Yet, he also knew all these things had to happen. Therefore, he threw himself on the ground and prayed these words, asking God to save him from the certain death awaiting him. But even in the midst of his fear, his doubt, and his uncertainty, Jesus knew it was God's will for him to die. Thus, he willingly went forward to meet his fate. He believed whole-heartedly that the will of his Father must prevail and that what God wanted for him was what mattered, not what his own will would have preferred. God knows all, sees all, and directs all, and Jesus knew the plan for his life was in the hands of his Father.

When we are in the midst of trials and tribulations, we often pray to God to "remove this cup" from us, not realizing that we may be experiencing these things for a reason. We must trust in God's will for us and have a deep, abiding faith that everything that happens to us is part of God's master plan for our lives.

If we give our lives over to God's will, rather than constantly trying to impose our own will, we will begin to find that some events make us stronger and more spiritually mature. For how can we grow when everything is handed to us easily and effortlessly and when all is going well? It is in our trials that we are molded and shaped into more than we ever imagined we could be, as clay in the sculptor's hands. It is in our tribulations that our faith is solidified, like clay that is fired in the kiln.

"God's will, not our own." This is the message of Jesus' words. It is what he believed and what he calls us to believe.

praise You for Your sovereignty over the broad events of my life and over the details. With You, nothing is accidental, nothing is incidental, and no experience is wasted. You hold in Your own power my breath of life and all my destiny. And every trial that You allow to happen is a platform on which You reveal Yourself, showing Your love and power, both to me and to others looking on.

Ruth Myers, *31 Days of Praise*

Quiet My Heart

Lord, teach me to silence my own heart that I may listen to the gentle movement of the Holy Spirit within me and sense the depths which are of God.

Sixteenth-century Frankfurt prayer

This beautiful sixteenth-century prayer beckons us to follow the voice of the Lord for the guidance we crave. Often we let our emotions drown out his words to us. When we follow our feelings without consulting God, we end up overreacting or acting impulsively.

If we could learn to become still and pray while it is quiet, we might just hear something stirring deep within our hearts—a divine voice speaking to us.

If I am right, Thy grace impart,
Still in the right to stay;
If I am wrong, oh teach my heart
To find that better way.

Alexander Pope, "An Essay on Man"

Thy Will Be Done

~~~

Hear my prayer, O Lord; give ear to my supplications in your faithfulness; answer me in your righteousness. . . .

Save me, O Lord, from my enemies; I have fled to you for refuge. Teach me to do your will, for you are my God. Let your good spirit lead me on a level path.

For your name's sake, O Lord, preserve my life. In your righteousness bring me out of trouble.

Psalm 143:1, 9–11

Søren Kierkegaard once said, "Prayer does not change God, but it changes the one who prays." Sincere prayer does this by changing our "my will be done" into "thy will be done," even as Christ himself taught us to pray when he prayed these works prior to his arrest and execution.

Eventually we all have to pray a prayer like the one the psalmist prayed. It is a prayer for God to teach us the way we should go, to teach us to do his will, and to let his good Spirit lead us on a level path.

~~~

Be joyful always; pray continually; give thanks in all circumstances, for this is God's will for you in Christ Jesus.

1 Thessalonians 5:16–18 NIV

~~~

The Lord is always eager to guide us in every area of our lives, and when we pray this way, the Holy Spirit teaches us how to love God and to love others. Now that's a life-changing prayer.

I believe that God's true will is that men should love one another and should consequently do to others as they wish others to do to them—of which it is said in the Gospels that in this is the law and the prophets.

Leo Tolstoy

In God's Sight

In the midst of the darkness that threatens to overwhelm us lies a pinpoint of light, a persistent flicker that guides us through the pain and fear, through the hopelessness and despair, to a place of peace and healing on the other side. This is God's Spirit, leading us back home.

Heavenly Father, in you we live and move and have our being: We humbly pray you will guide and govern us by your Holy Spirit, that in all the cares and occupations of our life we may not forget you, but may remember that we are ever walking in your sight; through Jesus Christ our Lord. Amen.

Book of Common Prayer

What does it mean to "remember" that we are ever in God's sight? For this day, let it be a gentle reminder that smiling heavenly eyes rest upon your shoulders, no matter where you are, no matter the problems you face.

God's loving Spirit is always with us, ready to take our hands and lead us through this life to the eternal life in the Lord's heavenly kingdom.

Breakfast With God

Let me hear of your steadfast love in the morning, for in you I put my trust. Teach me the way I should go, for to you I lift up my soul.

Psalm 143:8

The first thing we think about in the morning should be the love of God. If we start by remembering that he loves us, we will trust him. Then we will worship him. And then we will do his will. Not a bad plan.

Have you had your morning psalm? Serve it up before breakfast, and taste the glory and the goodness of God. Everything else goes down better after that. Think of it as a vitamin for the soul, fortifying your desire to spend your day in service to our Lord.

Devotion is a certain act of the will by which man gives himself promptly to the service of God.

Thomas Aquinas

Trusting God

Do not let your hearts be troubled, and do not let them be afraid.

John 14:27

My Lord God, I have no idea where I am going. I do not see the road ahead of me. I cannot know for certain where it will end. Nor do I really know myself, and the fact that I think I am following your will does not mean I am actually doing so. But I believe that the desire to please you does in fact please you. And I hope I have that desire in all that I am doing. I hope that I will never do anything apart from that desire. And I know that if I do this you will lead me by the right road, though I may know nothing about it. Therefore I will trust you always though I may seem to be lost and in the shadow of death. I will not fear, for you are ever with me, and you will never leave me to face my perils alone.

Thomas Merton

When we don't know what's going on, it's nice to know who's in charge. And it's even better to know God is on our side. Regardless of our fears, we can do our best and trust the Lord.

In this prayer, Thomas Merton, a Trappist monk who helped many others lead a life of contemplation, taps into a deeper truth. God accepts us where we are, even when we don't know who we are or what he wants. We can have confidence that our desire to please God pleases God.

For Merton, desire is the thing we offer. If we desire God in everything, he will find us even when we feel lost.

In fact, he never left us. And he never will.

Without faith it is impossible to please God, for whoever would approach him must believe that he exists and that he rewards those who seek him.

Hebrews 11:6

Look to the Lord

Be Thou my guardian and my Guide
And hear me when I call:
Let not my slippery footsteps slide,
And hold me lest I fall.

The world, the flesh and Satan dwell
Around the path I tread:
O save me from the snares of hell,
Thou Quickener of the dead.

And if I am tempted to sin,
And outward things are strong,
Do Thou O Lord, keep watch within,
And save my soul from wrong.

Still let me ever watch and pray,
And feel that I am frail;
That if the Tempter cross my way,
Yet he may not prevail.
Amen.

Book of Common Prayer

Sing out in joyful praise, for we have a guardian and a guide who holds us up should we not be able to walk on our own! We have a Savior watching out for us along the path when temptation and sin come calling. We have an inner resource to tap into when the outer world threatens to snare us, as this beautiful hymn tells us.

When we look to God to do for us all the things we cannot do for ourselves, our footsteps are made sure, our path is made straight, and our way is made clear. When we pray to God to keep us from wrongdoing and sin, we are strengthened and emboldened to continue on the path to even greater achievements and opportunities.

In moments of confusion, fear, and doubt, it is empowering to know that we can always pray to God for a helping hand and a shoulder to lean on. Imagine what wonderful things we could experience in our lives that we may have been avoiding because we were too afraid to "go it alone." How glorious it is to know we are never really going it alone at all! Indeed, we have a constant companion along the path of life who is accessible to us any time we choose to pray.

Always With Us

Dear Jesus, we know there is no greater burden than to think no one cares or understands. That is why the promise of your presence is so precious to us, you who said, "Remember, I am with you always, to the end of the age."

Delight in His Will

I delight to do thy will, O my God: yea, thy law is within my heart.

Psalm 40:8 KJV

A great secret is in this prayer for those who want to know and do the will of God. That secret is to simply love God and do his will.

It's not that complicated. But then again, it's not that easy. We have to delight in his will so much that we fill our hearts with his Word. When we do that, we can concentrate on doing what we already know instead of worrying about what we don't know.

In fact, sometimes we don't even have to pray about the will of God. We just have to follow it. Nevertheless, praying will always make it easier.

Persistent Prayer

Then Gideon said to God, "In order to see whether you will deliver Israel by my hand, as you have said, I am going to lay a fleece of wool on the threshing floor; if there is dew on the fleece alone, and it is dry on all the ground, then I shall know that you will deliver Israel by my hand, as you have said." And it was so. When he rose early next morning and squeezed the fleece, he wrung enough dew from the fleece to fill a bowl with water. Then Gideon said to God, "Do not let your anger burn against me, let me speak one more time; let me, please, make trial with the fleece just once more; let it be dry only on the fleece, and on all the ground let there be dew." And God did so that night. It was dry on the fleece only, and on all the ground there was dew.

Judges 6:36–40

This is a prayer strategy that should come with a warning: "Don't try this at home." Many people have tested God with such prayers, and not all have had Gideon's success. In fact, Moses specifically told the children of Israel, "Do not put the Lord thy God to the test." The context was their demand for God to give them the thing they wanted: the pleasures of Egypt in the Sinai desert.

It's tempting to assume that the Lord should make things easy, especially for us. Gideon's prayer was desperate, however, not presumptuous. It was not about something he wanted, but about something he didn't want—the responsibility of leading his people.

The tribes of Israel were under siege, and when the angel of the Lord appeared to him and called him a "mighty warrior," it was almost laughable. Gideon was a small man from a small family, threshing wheat in an ancient winepress so the Midianites wouldn't steal it from him.

If ever anyone needed a sign, Gideon was the man. And that's what he asked for. God was asking him to lead a frightened nation against a frightening army, and he wanted to know for sure that God was doing the asking. Most of the time when we test God, we are looking for direction. Gideon was looking for assurance. It was a great task to which he was called, and he needed a great God.

He had the right attitude when he made this request— that is, asking with reverence and fear. He had the courage to

Let us then approach the throne of grace with confidence, so that we may receive mercy and find grace to help us in our time of need.

Hebrews 4:16 NIV

be honest with God, and it changed his life. This timid, reluctant farmer became a leader, a soldier, and a judge. And while he was not presumptuous, he was persistent.

Centuries later, Jesus praised the widow who kept pestering the unjust judge until he did the right thing. This parable, Luke tells us, was intended to "teach us to pray and not give up."

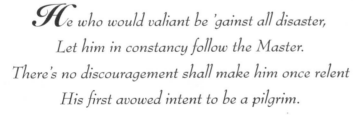

In the face of great adversity, Gideon knew what to do: to be bold before God, and to be willing to ask again.

He who would valiant be 'gainst all disaster,
Let him in constancy follow the Master.
There's no discouragement shall make him once relent
His first avowed intent to be a pilgrim.

John Bunyan

The Ship of Life

Steer the ship of my life, good Lord, to your quiet harbor, where I can be safe from the storms of sin and conflict. Show me the course I should take. Renew in me the gift of discernment, so that I can always see the right direction in which I should go. And give me the strength and the courage to choose the right course, even when the sea is rough and the waves are high, knowing that through enduring hardship and danger in your name we shall find comfort and peace.

Basil of Caesarea

Basil of Caesarea (c. 330–379) did indeed let the Lord steer his ship, giving up a promising career in public life to become first a monk and then a bishop in Eastern Asia Minor. He built schools and hospitals for the poor and the sick, caring particularly for lepers and other outcasts of society. In one of many prayers composed by this deeply religious man, Basil compares life to a ship and asks that the Lord be the one to plot his course.

When we ask God to take over the ship of our own lives, we know not only that we will be led in the right direction but also that we will be protected through the roughest of times. God's intention is to lead us to a peaceful shore, where our destiny awaits, if we are willing to give up control and let God be the wind that fills our sails.

Flying in Formation

We're tempted to give up until we see the example of geese. When they fly, they fly in a "V" formation with the leading goose providing wind resistance for those who follow. When the leading goose tires, another goose takes a turn as the leading goose to keep the flock moving onward. When we tire and need God's help, he is always there to take the point position for us so we can keep moving forward.

God's Sweet Word

I treasure your word in my heart, so that I may not sin against you. . . . I will delight in your statutes; I will not forget your word. . . . Then I shall have an answer for those who taunt me, for I trust in your word.

Psalm 119:11, 16, 42

Thy law is perfect, Lord of light; Thy testimonies sure; The statutes of thy realm are right, And thy commands are pure.

James Montgomery

The Word of God is sweet to the taste. In fact, both Ezekiel and John were given scrolls to eat, which were sweeter than honey. And we are also told that God's Word is more precious than silver or fine gold.

I wonder, then, why I don't take God more seriously? Why I don't serve his Word for breakfast? Why I don't hide it in my heart? I wonder, if I did, would it change me? The answer, of course, is that it would. God's Word would turn my will in the direction of God's will, and it would make me be more like his precious Son, Jesus Christ.

The Sea of Faith

O Lord, sea of love and goodness, let me not fear too much the storms and winds of my daily life, and let me know that there is ebb and flow but that the sea remains the sea.

Henri Nouwen

Battling the stormy times in our lives can certainly be frightening. Henri Nouwen, a priest who gave up a promising clerical career to work in a home for the mentally challenged, must often have faced the cruel waves of discouragement. For him, as for us, it's only natural to pray for deliverance from fear. Yet, if we believe that God oversees the storm and that he cares for those who feel its terror, we can also rest assured that we will arrive at just the right destination.

Seeking courage, Lord, I bundle my fears and place them in your hands.

Asking for Wisdom

O God, by whom the meek are guided in judgment, and light rises up in darkness for the godly: Grant us, in all our doubts and uncertainties, to ask what you would have us do; that the spirit of wisdom may save us from all false choices, that in your light we may see light, and in your straight paths we may not stumble, through Jesus Christ our Lord, who lives and reigns with you and the Holy Spirit, one God, for ever and ever.

Book of Common Prayer

Joan of Arc is best known for leading soldiers into battle and being burned at the stake for her faith in Christ. There are books, plays, movies, and Web sites about her. Most of the stories about her are true. Although this prayer is associated with her, it's possible she did not say it.

Whatever legends and myths surrounded her life, one thing is fairly clear: She was a simple young woman of simple faith who constantly prayed for God to give her wisdom. She deeply felt the responsibility of leadership, and she wanted to make the right choices for those who depended on her.

Most of us will never be recognized as a heroic saint as Joan was. Nevertheless, all of us have responsibility for others: our kids, our parents, our coworkers. And we all have battles of our own.

Asking for wisdom, as this prayer does, is something all of us can do, and should do, for only God's wisdom will steer us on the right course.

Take my instruction instead of silver, and knowledge rather than choice gold; for wisdom is better than jewels, and all that you may desire cannot compare with her.

Proverbs 8:10–11

The Twenty-Third Psalm

The Next Step

Lord, give me the faith to take the next step even when I don't know what lies ahead. Give me the assurance that even if I stumble and fall, you'll pick me up and put me back on the right path.

And give me the confidence that, even if I lose faith, you will never lose me.

The Lord is my shepherd, I shall not want. He makes me lie down in green pastures; he leads me beside still waters; he restores my soul. He leads me in right paths for his name's sake.

Even though I walk through the darkest valley, I fear no evil; for you are with me; your rod and your staff— they comfort me.

You prepare a table before me in the presence of my enemies; you anoint my head with oil; my cup over-flows. Surely goodness and mercy shall follow me all the days of my life, and I shall dwell in the house of the Lord my whole life long.

Psalm 23

This psalm of David has become one of the most loved prayers of all time, and it has given spiritual hope and assur-ance to millions of Jews and Christians. Within its beautiful, poetic imagery lies a message of good news—that we are loved and protected by a God who is always with us, even when we walk through life's darkest valleys.

That we are like sheep in the hands of a good and caring shepherd makes us feel a sense of safety in an often unsafe world. We are told in this psalm that if we are in need of something, the Lord will provide it so that our cup overflows. We are told that if we seek serenity, restoration, anointing, prosperity, and right action, the Lord will provide them as well, and as he does, we will walk in lovely "green pastures" beside "still waters."

We are also told that "goodness and mercy" shall surely follow us if we stay close to the Lord and that we will forever dwell in the Lord's house if we choose to follow his lead. What a wonderful promise of blessings. And all we are asked to do is be like good sheep and allow our beloved shepherd to take care of us.

Psalm 23 has changed and empowered lives by providing a shield of protection and comfort for those who suffer and are afraid. We are told to fear no evil, for God stands before us in the face of any adversity. The shadows of darkness cannot harm us when the Lord is on our side. And the Lord is always on our side, for his light casts away all shadows from our lives.

Yet, even for those who do not suffer or face a certain evil, Psalm 23 is a blessing that warms the heart and reassures the soul, for it tells us that we are being watched over at all times, good and bad, by a God who dearly loves us and wants nothing more than our happiness and joy.

Our only task is to keep step with him. He chooses the direction and leads the way. As we walk step by step with him, we soon discover that we have lost the crushing burden of needing to take care of ourselves and get our own way, and we discover that the burden is indeed light. We come into the joyful, simple life of hearing and obeying.

Richard Foster, *Freedom of Simplicity*

Everlasting Gifts

O God, You are our Creator.
You are good and Your mercy knows no bounds.
To You arises the praise of every creature.
O God, You have given us an inner law by which
we must live.
To do Your will is our task.
To follow Your ways is to know peace of heart.
To You we offer our homage.
Guide us on all the paths we travel upon
this earth.
Free us from all the evil tendencies which
lead our hearts away from Your will.
Never allow us to stray from You.
Give us true joy and authentic love, and a
lasting solidarity among peoples.
Give us Your everlasting gifts. Amen!

Pope John Paul II

This prayer teaches us that God can give us the vital things we
need to walk faithfully with him: a clear conscience, a peaceful

heart, a true joy, an authentic love, a lasting solidarity, and everlasting gifts.

The clear conscience comes from knowing and doing what God has asked us to do. He has given us "an inner law," and following his will, as Pope John Paul II says, is "our task." Everything else flows from the goodness and mercy of God, which "knows no bounds." In fact, all of the rest—the peace, love, joy, and unity—can be counted among the "everlasting gifts" in the last line of his prayer.

God does give us many wonderful gifts. In fact, the Book of James tells us that every good and perfect gift is from God's hands, and these are the gifts that will change our lives and transform our characters.

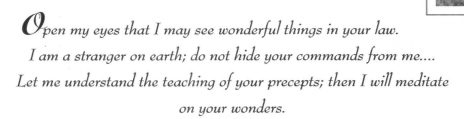

Open my eyes that I may see wonderful things in your law.
I am a stranger on earth; do not hide your commands from me....
Let me understand the teaching of your precepts; then I will meditate
on your wonders.

Psalm 119:18–19, 27 NIV

Mother Teresa's Prayer

Lord, open our eyes, that we may see you in our brothers and sisters.

Lord open our ears, that we may hear the cries of the hungry, the cold, the frightened, the oppressed.

Lord open our hearts, that we may love each other as you love us.

Renew in us your spirit, Lord.

Free us and make us one.

Mother Teresa

Listening can be a better service than speaking.

Dietrich Bonhoeffer,
Life Together

Few people have heard the cries of the hungry, the cold, and the frightened the way Mother Teresa did. And none, perhaps, have done so much in response.

Although she had a secure and rewarding ministry as a missionary school teacher in India, she decided to leave her convent to live among the poorest of the poor. Her years of sacrificial service did not go unnoticed, and she won the Nobel Peace Prize in 1979 in addition to many other awards and much acclaim.

Rejoice with those who rejoice; mourn with those who mourn.

Romans 12:15 NIV

Nevertheless, the charity work she did and believed in humbled her. It is a fact that we gain far more from the poor than they gain from us. "They give us much more than we give them," she said, remembering when she had gone out into the streets of Calcutta and brought back a dying woman. She cared for the woman herself, but as she cleaned her and put her to bed, the woman clasped her hand, smiled, and said, "Thank you." Then she died.

This incident moved Mother Teresa. She said if she were dying, she would try to bring attention to herself. "I would have said: I am hungry or I am cold or I am dying. But this woman was so great, she was so beautiful in her giving."

"The poor are great people," Mother Teresa repeated over and over again. "They do not need our sympathy and our pity. They need our love and compassion."

Mother Teresa's request for God to help her to help others changed her life. It can do the same for us.

Teach me to feel another's woe,
To hide the fault I see;
That mercy I to others show,
That mercy show to me.

Alexander Pope, "An Essay on Man"

The Armor of Light

~

The night is far gone, the day is near. Let us then lay aside the works of darkness and put on the armor of light; let us live honorably as in the day.

Romans 13:12–13

Sometimes, during my travels, I request a wake-up call, but I'm seldom still asleep when it comes. I'm already up, excited about the possibilities of a new place with new things to do. I dress quickly, eager to see what the day has in store.

I should approach every day this way. I should put on the armor of light, greeting the day with new energy and greater devotion. We are to "live honorably as in the day," excited about the prospect of knowing and doing the will of God.

If we wish to make any progress in the service of God, we must begin every day of our life with new ardor.

Charles Cardinal Borromeo

~

To Give Freely

Lord, teach me to be generous.
Teach me to serve you as you deserve;
to give and not to count the cost,
to fight and not to heed the wounds,
to toil and not to seek for rest,
to labor and not to ask for reward,
save that of knowing that I do your will.

St. Ignatius

Giving should be a celebration of love.

Ignatius Loyola was a generous and devoted Jesuit priest, who served God in innumerable ways. Yet, he still felt the need to ask God how he could be of even greater service, and he never asked for or expected any reward in return for his actions. He was willing to put aside his own needs for the needs of others in order to faithfully serve God.

When we examine our own lives, do we find that our giving has come with a price? Has our work been performed only for what we could gain from it? Did we serve others without asking to be served in return? By looking closely at our own capacity for unconditional love and giving, we may find we are sorely lacking in generosity of spirit.

By focusing on the needs of others and by giving without expecting something in return, we will be doing God's will, and our lives will take on new meaning, purpose, and direction. Ignatius understood how to truly follow the Lord, and now we can, too. Doing God's will for no other reason than to please him is the greatest reward of all.

God wants us to do good deeds as an expression of the love God has put in our hearts.

God's Challenges

But he said, "O my Lord, please send someone else."
Then the anger of the Lord was kindled against
Moses and he said, "What of your brother Aaron, the
Levite? I know that he can speak fluently."

Exodus 4:13–14

When Moses spoke with God at the "burning bush," he was not prepared for the mission God was about to give him. Moses doubted his ability as a leader, a speaker, and a warrior for the Lord. Nevertheless, the Lord would not accept his doubts. In no uncertain terms, God told Moses he was going to lead the Israelites out of slavery in Egypt. God's plan was to speak through Moses, who in turn would speak through Aaron, his brother, for Aaron was a great orator. This way, God's message would make its way to the people, and Moses would come to be one of Israel's greatest leaders.

We do not have to be up to the cause when a challenge first presents itself, for that is where God comes in. With God, we discover the inner resources we thought we lacked. With God, we find the abilities we doubted we are capable of. With God, there is no need to "send someone else." God will help us

meet any challenge he gives us. With God, we can do anything, achieve anything, and overcome anything, because He will always empower us.

Let go and let God see you through.
Give in and let God be with you.
Surrender to a love that heals all things.
Let go and let God be your wings.

In Christ's Footsteps

Almighty, eternal, just and merciful God, grant us the desire to do only what pleases you, and the strength to do only what you command. Cleanse our souls, enlighten our minds, and inflame our hearts with your Holy Spirit, that we may follow in the footsteps of your beloved Son, Jesus Christ.

St. Francis of Assisi

Let Your Light Shine

Do you want to "shine like a star"? If you do, be sure your relationship with Christ makes a difference in the way you live.

Francis of Assisi is known best for his two prayers "Lord, Make Me An Instrument of Your Peace" and "Brother Sun, Sister Moon." In this prayer, however, he shares more of his insight about Christ. He offers us a wonderful opportunity to reconnect with the Holy Spirit, which enlightens us in how to faithfully walk with Jesus Christ.

When we make the choice to live according to God's

will, we know that we will also be given the fortitude and courage needed to change what is not working in our lives. God never gives us an opportunity without also providing us with a way to make it work. Nor does God ever give us a command we are not empowered to obey. If we truly want to change our lives, all we have to do is ask and then follow the path that Jesus has paved for us.

O Master, let me walk with Thee
In lowly paths of service free;
Tell me Thy secret; help me bear
The strain of toil, the fret of care.
Help me the slow of heart to move
By some clear, winning word of love;
Teach me the wayward feet to stay,
And guide them in the homeward way.

Washington Gladden, "O Master, Let Me Walk with Thee"

God's Light

Your word is a lamp to my feet and a light to my path.

Psalm 119:105

My wife likes to sleep with the light on, and I like to sleep with it off. When either of us has to get up in the middle of the night, however, we both agree that a night-light is good. Yet, during the day, even when the sun is shining, we both like to have bright lights on indoors in order to see.

Meanwhile, only God's Word provides the light we need to follow God's will.

Man is a weak and miserable animal until the light of God burns in his soul. But when that light burns…man becomes the most powerful being in the world. Nor can this be otherwise, for what then acts in him is no longer his strength but the strength of God.

Leo Tolstoy

Day by Day

May I know You more clearly,
Love You more dearly,
And follow You more nearly,
Day by day.

Richard of Chichester

The Lord is near to
all who call on him.

Psalm 145:18

Richard of Chichester studied at Oxford and Paris before becoming chancellor of Oxford University in 1235. Then, in 1244, he began a new era of his life, becoming the Bishop of Chichester. There he decided on a lifelong goal of elevating the level of spirituality among the people in his area.

Richard's poetic prayer gives evidence of his heartfelt desire to walk closely with God. These words were put to song some years ago, and they retain their life-changing power to this day. If we were to offer the sentiments of this simple prayer each morning, desiring to follow his will, we would surely grow in our sense of God's abiding nearness.

Crying for Mercy

~~~~~~~~~

The tax collector, standing far off, would not even look up to heaven, but was beating his breast and saying, "God, be merciful to me, a sinner!"

Luke 18:13

A Contrite Heart

~~~

The sacrifice acceptable to God is a broken spirit; a broken and contrite heart, O God, you will not despise.

Psalm 51:17

The Lord is gracious and righteous; our God is full of compassion. The Lord protects the simplehearted; when I was in great need, he saved me.

Psalm 116:5–6 NIV

David prayed this prayer soon after the prophet Nathan confronted him about his adulterous affair with Bathsheba and his murder of her husband, Uriah. It's an amazing prayer, for it teaches us that God is a forgiving God no matter how badly we behave. Indeed, we see David at his worst, and yet God still forgave him because David truly repented of his sins.

I remember being in college, involved in relationships every bit as self-serving as David's, full of my own strength and ambition. I was no Hebrew king, of course, but the same forces and reasons motivated me. After a car accident, for which I was at fault, and in which others were seriously hurt, I was flat on my back, broken physically.

It was then that I discovered this prayer and made it my own. Lying there, considering the consequences of my actions, I offered God what David offered God—a broken and contrite heart.

God then offered me the same thing he offered David— a fresh start.

The one whose love and wisdom we question is at our side, reading our thoughts and knowing as no other. He silently pursues the beneficial end of the trial and sorrow He permits. . . . Our heavenly Father, who corrects us because He loves us, is too wise to err in His government of our lives, and too good to err through malice. Therefore, we can safely trust ourselves to His care.

Herbert Lockyer, *Dark Threads the Weaver Needs*

Sincere Repentance

The tax collector, standing far off, would not even look up to heaven, but was beating his breast and saying, "God, be merciful to me, a sinner!"

Luke 18:13

The saints are the sinners who keep on trying.

Robert Louis Stevenson

One day when Jesus encountered people who regarded themselves as righteous and others with contempt, he told a parable about two people who went to the temple to pray. The first man was a Pharisee who listed reasons why he was spiritually superior to others. The other man was a tax collector who acknowledged his sinfulness before God and cried out for forgiveness. Jesus then noted that it was the tax collector, not the Pharisee, whom God justified.

In this parable, Jesus reminds us that even the most sinful among us will be shown God's mercy, if we but ask for it. God will always forgive us when we come to him with the sincere desire to be forgiven, no matter how we've sinned.

Prayer for Healing

Heal me, O Lord, and I shall be healed; save me, and I shall be saved; for you are my praise.

Jeremiah 17:14

The prophet Jeremiah faced many tough times while calling his people back to God. He endured taunting, exile, imprisonment, and all manner of harsh treatment because he always turned to God for help. What Jeremiah needed most from God, however, was spiritual healing, and he knew God would offer that as well.

We, too, need healing—even those of us who proclaim the gospel near and far. And when the Lord does heal us, we are truly healed now and forever.

We shall look up, lift up our heads, and look for the coming King.
With his coming will come also complete wholeness
and vibrant health.

Mildred Tengbom, *Why Waste Your Illness?*

The Blessing of Need

Lord, I am in need, be pleased to supply me; but, meanwhile, if you do not, I believe it is better for me to be in need, and so I praise you for my necessity while I ask you to supply it. I glory in my infirmity, even while I ask you to overcome it. I bless you for my affliction even while I ask you to help me in it and to rescue me out of it.

Charles Spurgeon

The nineteenth-century British pastor Charles Spurgeon was called "The Prince of Preachers." He is also the author of a 63-volume collection of his sermons, which is the largest set of books by a single writer in the history of Christianity.

He began his ministry at the age of 20 as pastor of the New Park Street Church in London, and he eventually preached to crowds of over 10,000, long before the days of amplifiers. He was known as a humble person with a sense of humor and a love for the downcast of society.

Both Spurgeon and his wife Susanna suffered from health problems. In his case, it was severe gout. He often preached in great pain, and he died at the early age of 58.

It is no wonder then that in this prayer he asked for help with his physical "infirmity." What is a wonder is that he gloried in it and blessed God for it! Spurgeon had absolute confidence in God's will—even if it was not what he himself wanted.

Our lives would also change if we trusted God as much as Spurgeon did. If we did, others would also be drawn to a life of faith in Christ.

Likewise the Spirit helps us in our weakness; for we do not know how to pray as we ought, but that very Spirit intercedes with sighs too deep for words.

Romans 8:26

Simple Deliverance

⁓⁓

I love the Lord, because he has heard my voice and my supplications. Because he inclined his ear to me, therefore I will call on him as long as I live. The snares of death encompassed me; the pangs of Sheol laid hold on me; I suffered distress and anguish. Then I called on the name of the Lord: "O Lord, I pray, save my life!"

Gracious is the Lord, and righteous; our God is merciful. The Lord protects the simple; when I was brought low, he saved me. Return, O my soul, to your rest, for the Lord has dealt bountifully with you.

Psalm 116:1–7

He gives power to the faint, and strengthens the powerless.

Isaiah 40:29

In this prayer, David recalled how the Lord had answered his previous prayer, as well as the one before that. In fact, because God had heard and answered his prayers in the past, David was determined to call on God as long as he lived.

David had prayed during the darkest moments of his young life when King Saul hunted him and while he hid in the caves of Judea. He lived the life of a fugitive, forced at times to seek shelter with the traditional enemies of his own people. He felt the pain of hell, he said, and suffered both anguish and distress.

Nevertheless, David was convinced that a gracious, righteous, and merciful God had saved him whenever he called out for deliverance. Ultimately, he received more than he asked for; he received a throne of his own and the promise of a bright future.

I often wonder what changed his life, and I find part of the answer in this prayer. He says the Lord protects the simple,

> *The greatest truths are the simplest, and so are the greatest men.*
>
> A. W. Hare

and his own prayer for deliverance had been basic: He called out in faith for God to save him, and God did.

That seems quite simple. Indeed, we are called to simple faith. Jesus himself said on three different occasions, "Anyone who will not receive the kingdom of God like a little child will never enter it."

That must have been how David prayed, with the need and the faith of a child. He then discovered that the Lord protects the simple and answers their prayers.

There's a wideness in God's mercy,
like the wideness of the sea;
There's a kindness in his justice,
which is more than liberty.
For the love of God is broader
Than the measure of man's mind;
And the heart of the Eternal
Is most wonderfully kind.
If our love were but more simple,
We should take him at his word:
And our lives would all be sunshine
In the sweetness of our Lord.

Frederick Faber

Earnest Entreaties

Grant, we beseech Thee, Almighty God, that we may so please Thy Holy Spirit by our earnest entreaties, that we may by His grace both be freed from all temptations and merit to receive the forgiveness of our sins. Through Christ our Lord, Amen.

From the Roman Missal

To err is human; to forgive, divine.

Alexander Pope

There is nothing so empowering as God's grace; it brings us freedom from evil and forgiveness for our past sins. In prayer, we offer up our "earnest entreaties," appealing for God's mercy and knowing God will answer our request.

The power of forgiveness lies in its ability to free us from the weight of past resentments, anger, and conflict. It makes us feel lighter and more open to life. Forgiveness heals, and that healing begins when we first go to God for redemption and renewal.

Help From the Lord

I lift up my eyes to the hills—from where will my help come? My help comes from the Lord, who made heaven and earth.

He will not let your foot be moved; he who keeps you will not slumber. . . .

The Lord will keep your going out and your coming in from this time on and forevermore.

Psalm 121:1–3, 8

Each year, the children of Israel ascended the mountains toward Jerusalem for the Holy Days. As they climbed the narrow, rocky trails, they would recite this prayer together.

They looked around them at the idols in the altars in the high places along the road, and they reminded themselves that their own help came from the Lord, who made the mountains in the first place. Then they asked the Lord to keep them from falling off the steep and winding trail. They also asked the Lord to protect them from the bandits who hid beside the trail in the dark shadows of the night.

It was a practical prayer about common problems. Fortunately, they were praying to a practical God, who promised to show them mercy and who did. Likewise, God's promised mercy is upon us as well.

Then pealed the bells more loud and deep:
"God is not dead; nor doth He sleep;
The wrong shall fail,
The right prevail,
With peace on earth, good will to men."

Henry Wadsworth Longfellow, "Christmas Bells"

A Prayer of Confession

~~~

Most merciful God, we confess that we have sinned against you in thought, word, and deed, by what we have done, and by what we have left undone. We have not loved you with our whole heart; we have not loved our neighbors as ourselves. We are truly sorry and we humbly repent.

For the sake of your Son Jesus Christ, have mercy on us and forgive us; that we may delight in your will, and walk in your ways, to the glory of your Name. Amen.

Book of Common Prayer

A writer once spoke of a very harrowing experience. He had left his only copy of four chapters of a new book in a hotel room drawer. When he called to retrieve that priceless stack of papers, the manager insisted that the chapters had been thrown away. The man was devastated. He thought of the months of energy that had gone into polishing those four chapters. He imagined trying to start over, trying to recover just the right words again, yet knowing it would be impossible. But then—salvation! Two weeks later a cleaning woman called to say she had found the papers. All was not lost!

The story of a lost manuscript reminds us that our spiritual salvation is first and foremost all about being unfaithful, about sinning, about being truly lost to begin with. Yes, that awareness must come first. Sometimes we forget our condition, or we attempt to rationalize our sins. Unfortunately, if we ignore our true state, we only weaken

In your hands, God of grace, failures can become feedback, and mistakes can simply be lessons in what doesn't work. Remind me that perfection means "suited to the task," not "without mistakes."

our understanding of what God's gracious search-and-rescue mission is all about.

At the same time, we must never become discouraged in the face of our inconsistent lives, our debilitating addictions, or our repeated failures at living faithfully. God has always been looking for people just like us. In fact, Jesus said he came to earth to rescue sinners with his message of love and reconciliation with God.

Offering a prayer of confession like this prayer is the first step in changing the entire direction of our lives. Often, when we walk away from a person or situation, the door immediately closes behind us and stays forever sealed tight. When we walk away from God and his will, however, there is always an opportunity to return.

Therefore, let us acknowledge our sins and cry for God's mercy. For only as we utter our confessions can we claim the priceless blessing of God's forgiveness.

When a child is hurt and bleeding, we pull that child close. I'm sure that's why God's movement is always toward us, inviting us to come to him even when we're doing our best to pull away. Yet, we can repent and embrace the wonderful grace that is waiting for us.

The Blessed Paradox

~

God our healer, whose mercy is like a refining fire, touch us with your judgment, and confront us with your tenderness; that, being comforted by you, we may reach out to a troubled world, through Jesus Christ.

Janet Morley

In this short but penetrating entreaty, Janet Morley uses paradox to help us comprehend how God deals with us. For example, she describes God's mercy as fire—something that can

both burn and refine. She also says God both confronts us and is tender toward us.

Most importantly, Morley reminds us that all our petitions can be made "through Jesus Christ." When we think of Christ, we see paradox in action. He came to save the world, but he primarily taught his disciples. He came to heal and comfort hurting people, yet he often went away by himself to meditate and pray.

Similarly, we can approach our lives with the blessed paradox of heaven. If we truly are to make a difference in this troubled world, we'll need to spend much time away from it—in prayer. Such quality time with God will make us better vessels of his goodness in the world.

It takes courage to turn to you for healing, Lord——to reach out from this darkness to touch the hem of your garment and ask for healing. Please give us the assurance that you will never forsake us in our times of need.

Restore Us

Restore us, O God; let your face shine, that we may be saved.

O Lord God of hosts, how long will you be angry with your people's prayers? You have fed them with the bread of tears, and given them tears to drink in full measure. You make us the scorn of our neighbors; our enemies laugh among themselves.

Restore us, O God of hosts; let your face shine, that we may be saved.

Psalm 80:3–7

The face of God is so bright that he would not even allow Moses to see it. In one incident when he passed by Moses, Moses could see only his back. Moses' own face then became so radiant that he had to wear a veil when he talked with the people.

After that, and after a thousand failures, the people wanted God's face to shine on them again. "Restore us, O God Almighty; make your face shine upon us, that we may be saved," they prayed. It's a request repeated seven times in the Book of Psalms. It's a request we should repeat ourselves, allowing the light of his glory to make our faces shine. A life of faith transforms our countenance so that we mirror the light of God in a dark world.

Indeed, Paul said about God that he made his light shine "in our hearts to give the light of the knowledge of the glory of God in the face of Jesus Christ" (2 Cor. 4:6).

The Lord bless you and keep you; the Lord make his face shine upon you and be gracious to you; the Lord turn his face toward you and give you peace.

Numbers 6:24–26 NIV

Do Not Forget Me

O Lord! Thou knowest how busy I must be this day: if I forget thee, do not thou forget me.

Jacob Astley

We all lead busy lives, and we often forget to pray. We forget to give thanks. We forget to acknowledge God as our source of all that is good in our lives.

Sir Jacob Astley wrote this brief but powerful prayer before he was to partake in the Battle of Edgehill during the English Civil War. No doubt he desired the assurance that God would be with him in war, just as we desire the assurance that God will be with us when we need him. Although we may sometimes forget God, we are promised that God will never forget us.

Grant us wisdom,
Grant us courage,
For the facing of this hour,
For the facing of this hour.

Harry Emerson Fosdick, "God of Grace and God of Glory"

The New Man

O merciful God, grant that the old Adam in this child may be so buried, that the new man may be raised up in him.

Book of Common Prayer

This simple yet profound baptism prayer asks God to take away the sinner within us and replace it with a pure and innocent spirit. The "old Adam" is our old human nature, which is prone to sin and selfishness. The "new man" is our new nature, which seeks to please God and be like Christ.

When children are baptized, we ask that they be born anew in the Holy Spirit. But we can use this prayer even as adult Christians to help us as we struggle to turn from evil and sinful temptations.

The child is the father of the Man; And I could wish my days to be Bound each to each by natural piety.

William Wordsworth

Confessions and Forgiveness

O Lord, do not rebuke me in your anger, or discipline me in your wrath. For your arrows have sunk into me, and your hand has come down on me.

There is no soundness in my flesh because of your indignation; there is no health in my bones because of my sin. For my iniquities have gone over my head; they weigh like a burden too heavy for me. . . .

O Lord, all my longing is known to you; my sighing is not hidden from you. My heart throbs, my strength fails me; as for the light of my eyes—it also has gone from me. My friends and companions stand aloof from my affliction, and my neighbors stand far off. . . .

I am ready to fall, and my pain is ever with me. I confess my iniquity; I am sorry for my sin. Those who are *my foes without cause are mighty, and many are those who hate me wrongfully. Those who render me evil for good are my adversaries because I follow after good.*

Do not forsake me, O Lord; O my God, do not be far from me; make haste to help me, O Lord, my salvation.

Psalm 38:1–4, 9–11, 17–22

I consider myself as the most wretched of men, full of sores and corruption, and who has committed all sorts of crimes against his King. Touched with a sensible regret, I confess to Him all my wickedness, I ask His forgiveness, . . . The King, full of mercy and goodness, very far from chastising me, embraces me with love, makes me eat at His table, serves me with His own hands, gives me the key to His treasures; He converses and delights Himself with me incessantly, and treats me in all respects as His favorite.

Brother Lawrence,
The Practice of the Presence of God

For some, the path to God begins with confession—that is, acknowledging our weaknesses and failures while throwing ourselves on the mercy of God. But, it seems, confession has fallen out of fashion. In our world, guilt is considered a bad thing, and blame always belongs to someone else. It is a world where everyone is a victim and all of our troubles are someone else's fault, a world filled with pride and willfulness.

Yet, that is not the world where the saints lived, nor a place where the faithful people described in the Bible lived. Each of them at some point fell down before a holy and just God, and what they found in every instance was mercy and grace. This was the experience of David, who confessed his

weakness over and over again in this psalm while crying for God to deliver and save him.

Jesus teaches his followers to pray for the heavenly Father to "forgive us our sins." This shouldn't be too hard, considering that, as this prayer says, our longing is known to him and our sighing is not hidden. He already knows what our sins are. We are usually the ones who don't recognize them. Yet, seeing them, naming them, and turning from them are the first steps we take toward his throne. And we must take these steps with humility and strength.

If we confess our sins, he is faithful and just and will forgive us our sins and purify us from all unrighteousness.

1 John 1:9 NIV

At his throne we find forgiveness, and what we experience there is freedom. Confession seems like a small price to pay. All it costs us is our pride.

*O*ut of the depths I cry to thee;
Lord hear me, I implore thee.
Bend down they gracious ear to me;
Let my prayers come before thee.
On my misdeeds in mercy look,
O deign to blot them from thy book,
And let me come before thee.
Like those who watch for midnight's hour
To hail the dawning morrow,
I wait for thee, I trust thy power,
Unmoved by doubt or sorrow.
So let thy people hope in thee,
And they shall find thy mercy free,
And thy redemption plenteous.

Martin Luther, "Out of the Depths I Cry to Thee"

Who Is God?

Who is a God like you, pardoning iniquity and passing over the transgression of the remnant of your possession? He does not retain his anger forever, because he delights in showing clemency. He will again have compassion upon us; he will tread our iniquities under foot. You will cast all our sins into the depths of the sea.

Micah 7:18–19

There is no one holy like the Lord; there is no one besides you; there is no Rock like our God.

1 Samuel 2:2 NIV

The Hebrew prophet Micah asked a question that is good to ask at the beginning of any prayer. The answer is one that has occupied the prayers of God's people for centuries. He is a God who loves us, cares for us, waits for us, and forgives us; he is a God willing to cast all our sins into the sea.

Thinking about who God is—instead of thinking about what we want—changes our prayers. And ultimately it changes us.

The Powerful Cross

And behold: we who are standing beneath the cross of the ages, wish, through Your cross and passion, O Christ, to cry out today that mercy has irreversibly entered into the history of man, into our whole human history, and which, in spite of the appearances of weakness, is stronger than evil . . .

May the power of Your love once more be shown to be greater than the evil that threatens it. May it be shown to be greater than sin. . . . For by your blood and Your passion You have redeemed the world!

John Paul II

The cross is a powerful symbol of Christ's love. Nevertheless, as Pope John Paul II notes, the cross is also a symbol of power. The cross of Christ is stronger than evil and greater than sin. In fact, Jesus has redeemed the world through the cross.

This truth is transforming because a God who loved us so much that he would send his only Son to die for us will certainly leave a permanent mark on us through the cross. The apostle Paul reminded the Romans—and us—that "He who did not withhold his own Son, but gave him up for all of us, will he not with him also give us everything else?" (Rom. 8:32).

Everyday that we cry out for mercy and remind ourselves that Christ died for us is a day in which we remember that goodness will prevail—and that the Lord has already given us the ultimate mercy.

When I survey the wondrous cross
On which the Prince of Glory died,
My richest gains I count but loss,
And pour contempt on all my pride.
See, from his head, his hands, his feet,
Sorrow and love flow mingled down:
Did ever such love and sorrow meet,
Or thorns compose so rich a crown.

Isaac Watts

Jacob and Esau

~

Jacob said, "O God of my father Abraham and God of my father Isaac, O Lord who said to me, 'Return to your country and to your kindred, and I will do you good,' I am not worthy of the least of all the steadfast love and all the faithfulness that you have shown to your servant, for with only my staff I crossed this Jordan; and now I have become two companies. Deliver me, please, from the hand of my brother, from the hand of Esau, for I am afraid of him; he may come and kill us all, the mothers with the children. Yet you have said, 'I will surely do you good, and make your offspring as the sand of the sea, which cannot be counted because of their number.'"

Genesis 32:9–12

Jacob was afraid because he had cheated his brother, Esau, out of his birthright and blessing. Now that Jacob was bringing his family back to his homeland after years of exile, Esau was on his way to meet Jacob. Naturally Jacob did the only thing he could do—he pleaded for mercy by asking the Lord to spare his life and the lives of his family from his brother's expected wrath.

Imagine Jacob's immense surprise and relief when he finally encountered Esau, who not only forgave Jacob but also welcomed him with open arms! God answered Jacob's plea to be delivered from what seemed a certain death. In fact, God had made the situation even more positive than Jacob had even dared imagine.

How often do we imagine the worst? Yet, if we would just turn our lives over to God, we could have the best! We should remember this prayer the next time we assume something is going to turn out badly. Indeed, if we place our trust in God, as Jacob did, we may be pleasantly surprised by the outcome God has in store for us.

The Scripture keeps repeating this message to us: God is bigger than whatever you're afraid of.

Belief and Doubt

I believe; help my unbelief!

Mark 9:24

Sometimes we just aren't sure. We want to believe, but we can't. It doesn't seem to matter, though. God still hears our prayer for help.

A father whose child was troubled with evil spirits was the first person we know who prayed this prayer: "Help my unbelief." It is a prayer that has been prayed countless times since.

This desperate man possibly also said to Jesus, "If you can do anything, take pity on us and help us." Jesus saw the boy struggle with the demon and the man struggle with his faith, and he healed both of them, restoring speech to the child and faith to the father.

The disciples, who had tried to heal the boy, wanted to know why they couldn't cast the demon out of the boy. Jesus said to them, "This kind can come out only through prayer" (Mark 9:29). This statement shows how important prayer was to Jesus.

Guarding Our Eyes

Wondrously show your steadfast love, O savior of those who seek refuge from their adversaries at your right hand. Guard me as the apple of the eye; hide me in the shadow of your wings.

Psalm 17:7–8

"The apple of the eye" is an interesting image. We might confuse it with our appearing to God as an attractive piece of fruit. This Hebrew metaphor, however, actually refers to the pupil of the viewer's eye, and in this prayer it pertains to God's guarding us the same way people might shield their eyes from blowing sand, as well as being protected by his parental covering.

We are all quite careful about guarding our eyes. And God is quite careful about guarding our lives.

He sustained him in a desert land, in a howling wilderness waste; he shielded him, cared for him, guarded him as the apple of his eye.

Deuteronomy 32:10

I Am Not Worthy

I am not worthy, Holy Lord,
That Thou shouldst come to me:
Speak but the Word, one gracious Word,
Can set the sinner free.

I am not worthy: cold and bare
The lodging of my soul:
How canst Thou deign to enter there?
Lord, speak and make me whole.

Book of Common Prayer

When Jesus entered Capernaum, a Centurion approached him and appealed for a dying slave he deeply cared about. Being a Roman soldier, however, the Centurion did not feel worthy of Jesus' attention. In fact, he said to the Lord, "I am not worthy. . . but only speak the word, and let my servant be healed" (Luke 7:6–7).

This simple prayer of faith and belief so impressed Jesus that he turned

to the crowd of witnesses and declared, "I tell you, not even in Israel have I found such faith" (Luke 7:9). Jesus then healed the slave.

When we come to the Lord with the faith and humility of the Centurion at Capernaum, not only are we made worthy of his love and miracles, but those we love and care for are made worthy as well. Many times Jesus tried to tell his followers that faith was the key to joy and miracles, but not many of them truly understood. It took a Roman soldier, a natural enemy of the Jewish people, to have the kind of faith Jesus was talking about.

It takes great courage to reach out from the darkness of the world and touch the hem of the Lord's garment for healing. But for those who do, Jesus never disappoints.

Even though we are sinners, Christ still loves us. Even when we are weak, afraid, and lacking in self-esteem, Christ still loves us. In fact, nothing we can do can cause us to fall out of Christ's favor if we have sincere faith in him. If we go before Jesus with a humble, believing heart, we will be given a multitude of blessings in return. This is wonderful news for those times when we feel "less than" and "not enough." This is wonderful news for those times when we feel as though we don't deserve anything better than what we already have been given.

Jesus is trying to tell us that we will receive more, much more. In fact, we will receive the kingdom of God. Yet, some-

thing is first required of us, as the Centurion realized: We must ask; we must knock upon the door; and we must believe. Then, Jesus will answer.

Regardless of how unwanted and insignificant we may feel or how others may reject us, there is one who cares. Jesus spent little of his time in the citadels of power or networking with those who could promote his ministry with the religious and political leaders in Jerusalem. Though he turned no one away, more often than not he was found in the villages and countryside among the common people. Jesus' love for the poor and ordinary should be an inspiration to us all. We do not need to have wealth or success to have value in God's eyes.

I Seek Refuge

In you, O Lord, I seek refuge; do not let me ever be put to shame; in your righteousness deliver me. Incline your ear to me; rescue me speedily. Be a rock of refuge for me, a strong fortress to save me.

You are indeed my rock and my fortress; for your name's sake lead me and guide me, take me out of the net that is hidden for me, for you are my refuge.

Psalm 31:1–4

When I was about six, my dad pastored a little church on the side of a mountain in east Tennessee. Until then I had lived in south Florida, so the mountain itself was quite impressive. Yet, what I remember most were the rocks, one of which seemed almost as large as the cottage where we lived in nearby Chattanooga.

There were all kinds of hiding places, underneath, between, and in the sides of those rocks. After church, the kids played hide and seek, and we would often stay on the mountain for the entire afternoon. I remember being caught out in a storm once and feeling secure tucked under the cleft of a huge rock.

It was a safe place, a hiding place, sheltering me from both the wind and the rain. It was a place, the psalmist said, like God.

Rock of ages, cleft for me,
Let me hide myself in thee;
Let the water and the blood
From thy wounded side which flowed,
Be of sin the double cure,
Save from wrath and make me pure.

Augustas Toplady

He Hears You

I called on your name, O Lord, from the depths of the pit; you heard my plea, "Do not close your ear to my cry for help, but give me relief!" You came near when I called on you; you said, "Do not fear!" You have taken up my cause, O Lord, you have redeemed my life.

Lamentations 3:55–58

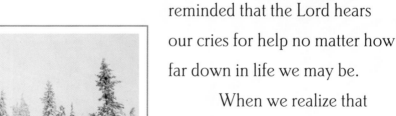

When you read God's word, you must constantly be saying to yourself, "It is talking to me, and about me."

Søren Kierkegaard

Isn't it great to know that God's steadfast love for us endures forever? This is what we are told in the third chapter of Lamentations, most notably in these verses, where we are reminded that the Lord hears our cries for help no matter how far down in life we may be.

When we realize that God does not turn a deaf ear to our prayers, we are confident that the Lord will reward our faithfulness. God tells us not to fear, for he has taken up our

cause. He will fight for us. He will stand with us. He will redeem us.

If you are at a low point in your life today, this powerful prayer of thanks and praise will empower you to have hope, for there is one who hears you and is there to reach out and help you rise from your pit of despair. That one is God, and he is always available to us when we cry out to him.

Along with life's blessings, there are also struggles, pain, and loss.
While we never welcome these things, we all must go through them.
At such times we most keenly feel our need for intervention,
and we call out to God.

A Clean Heart

~∾~

Create in me a clean heart, O God, and put a new and right spirit within me. Do not cast me away from your presence, and do not take your holy spirit from me. Restore to me the joy of your salvation, and sustain in me a willing spirit.

Psalm 51:10–12

In this prayer, King David pleads with God to forgive him for having committed adultery and murder. He is asking God for cleansing, wisdom, and renewal and to be molded with God's truth and salvation.

When we pray the 51st Psalm, we, too, can be restored and renewed, no matter what our past sins may have been. We are freed from the mistakes and transgressions that weigh us down through our willingness to be cleansed by the Holy Spirit. Though we may feel as though what we have done is unforgivable, God's mercy is ever available to us, just for the asking.

David's words speak of a longing to never be apart from God's presence and to experience the joy of salvation at the hands of a loving Creator. For God alone has the power to cleanse our hearts from sin, making them pure and holy.

O Lord, though I have disappointed you once again, you still shower me with your love and mercy. I am sorry for making the wrong decision. Guide me back to the path of righteousness so I might please and honor you.

Perfect in Weakness

◦~◦

Three times I appealed to the Lord about this, that it would leave me, but he said to me, "My grace is sufficient for you, for power is made perfect in weakness." So, I will boast all the more gladly of my weaknesses, so that the power of Christ may dwell in me.

2 Corinthians 12:8–9

Paul of Tarsus, the author of this letter (dated around A.D. 55) to the ancient Corinthian church, was known as the great "apostle to the Gentiles." He earned this title by establishing

and ministering to many churches throughout the Mediterranean world whose members were mostly Gentiles. Moving from one country to the next country over land and sea, he preached and taught the message of God's goodness and grace to anyone who would listen.

Paul himself was no stranger to the marvelous workings of God's grace in his own life. In referring to this prayer by Paul, some biblical historians claim that Paul must have suffered from a distressing malady. It may have been epilepsy or perhaps blindness.

Whatever Paul's particular weakness was, he affirms something in his cry for God's mercy that we can all take to heart: After asking God for relief, if it does not seem to come, we can assume that God's glory would be better served by a display of his power *in the midst of* our weaknesses. To be used by the Lord this way, Paul knew, is a great blessing. It's even something to "boast" about with thankfulness.

Lord, you are the light I follow down this long, dark tunnel. You are the hand that reaches out and grabs mine when I feel as though I am sinking in despair. I thank you, Lord, for although I may feel like giving up, you have not given up on me. Amen.

The Prayer of the Heart

Lord Jesus Christ, Son of God, have mercy on me, a sinner.

Known as "The Prayer of the Heart," this simple plea for Christ's mercy has its origins in the Greek Orthodox Church. Later, it became accessible to all Christians in the famous story of a man who wanted to learn to pray without ceasing, "The Way of a Pilgrim."

This prayer calls upon the name of the Lord, the Son of God, to show mercy upon the humble sinner. We are that humble sinner, wanting nothing more than to know God's will, feel God's love, and receive God's infinite blessings each and every day of our lives.

When Paul instructed the faithful at Thessalonica to "pray without ceasing" (1 Thess. 5:17), he knew the power of constant contact with God's mighty presence. For Christians, this call to daily prayer results in an ongoing communion with the Lord that reaches deep into the heart and soul to heal, to comfort, and to save. All sinners have access to this salvation. All we need to do is pray, "Lord Jesus Christ, Son of God, have mercy on me, a sinner," and the heart will soon open wide and begin to sing in grateful recognition of the nearness of God.

Jesus' love for every sinner should be an inspiration to us all. We do not have to have wealth or success to have value in God's eyes.

Prayers of Praise

My mouth will speak the praise of the Lord, and all flesh will
bless his holy name forever and ever.

Psalm 145:21

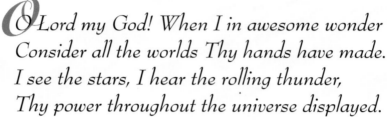

How Great Thou Art

O Lord my God! When I in awesome wonder
Consider all the worlds Thy hands have made.
I see the stars, I hear the rolling thunder,
Thy power throughout the universe displayed.

Then sings my soul, my Savior God, to Thee;
How great Thou art, how great Thou art!
Then sings my soul, my Savior God, to Thee;
How great Thou art, how great Thou art!

Carl Boberg

No one can deny the power of nature to inspire awe. That is what happened to Pastor Carl Boberg when he wrote these words of praise in 1886 while watching a raging thunderstorm soon give way to glorious sunny skies. So strong was the experience of nature's power that Boberg dropped to his knees in adoration of God. He then wrote a nine-stanza poem, which was put to the music of an old Swedish folk melody many years later.

Reading the hymn, we feel Boberg's passionate reminder that God is to be found in the details. If we do not slow down long enough to pay attention to a lovely summer day or a starry night sky, we not only miss the details but also the presence of our Creator, who permeates the universe. As Boberg tells us, God is not just in our churches but also in a roar of thunder, a flash of lightning, or a ray of golden sunlight breaking through a blanket of thick, gray clouds.

Nature makes the soul sing.

Small Miracles

Bless you, Lord! The heavens declare your glory; the skies proclaim your mighty power. And here I am, looking up into those vast regions, knowing that the tiniest cell in my body is a most glorious miracle, as well. Bless you, Lord!

Praise God

Praise God, from whom all blessings flow;
Praise Him all creatures here below;
Praise Him above, ye heavenly host;
Praise Father, Son, and Holy Ghost.

Thomas Ken

This prayerful song is one of the most frequently used pieces of music in public worship. Who could have imagined that this popular hymn was written for secret use during a time of religious intolerance and oppression?

Yet, that is the history of this doxology, the final stanza of a beautiful hymn called "Awake, My Soul, and with the Sun." In 1674, ordained Anglican priest Thomas Ken, who became Bishop of Bath and Wells in England in 1685, wrote this hymn at a time when the established church believed it blasphemous to write new lyrics for

Scripture-based church music. Ken penned the hymn for the boys at Winchester College to be used in secret for their own private devotions.

Ironically, history would soon see Ken's hymn of praise and worship become immensely popular with the public. It was even sung at his funeral.

The words speak of thanksgiving, gratitude, and the knowledge that God is the ultimate source of all blessings. While many prayers are supplicant in nature, this doxology did not ask God for anything but praised him for all things. It sup-

How good it is, Almighty One, to bask in the warmth of your love! Nothing more is needed than to receive your good gifts from above.

ports the statement made by Christ, who said, "Those who have would be given even more." Perhaps Ken knew Christ was referring to being grateful while recognizing that no matter what we need, God would provide, and provide in abundance.

When we praise God for what we have, what we have becomes even more. When we focus on what blessings we have already received, more blessings are sure to be showered upon us. Indeed, we are given all that we could ever want or could ever need.

That is the power of thanksgiving.

More things are wrought by prayer
Than this world dreams of.
Wherefore, let thy voice
Rise like a fountain for me night and day.
For what are men better than sheep or goats
That nourish a blind life within the brain,
If, knowing God, they lift not hands of prayer
Both for themselves and those who call them friend?
For so the whole round earth is every way
Bound by gold chains about the feet of God.

Alfred, Lord Tennyson, "Morte D'Arthur"

Difficult Blessings

I thank God for my handicaps, for through them, I have found myself, my work and my God.

Helen Keller

God is most glorified in us when we are most satisfied in him.

John Piper, *Desiring God*

Would it seem like a severe handicap to you to be unable to read this page? Would it be difficult for you to proceed through this day unable to hear, not even knowing the sound of your own voice?

Amazingly, Helen Keller gave thanks for such handicaps! Blind and deaf from the age of two, she struggled for years to learn what language was all about until the great day when she finally uttered her first word: "Water." Thereafter, she progressed rapidly, eventually graduating from Radcliffe in 1904 with honors. She went on to lecture around the world, raising funds for the training of the blind.

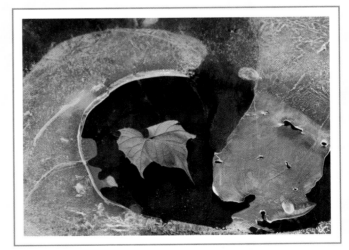

Jonah's Prayer

~~~~

Then Jonah prayed to the Lord his God from the belly of the fish, saying, "I called to the Lord out of my distress, and he answered me; out of the belly of Sheol I cried, and you heard my voice. You cast me into the

deep, into the heart of the seas, and the flood surrounded me; all your waves and your billows passed over me. Then I said, 'I am driven away from your sight; how shall I look again upon your holy temple?' The waters closed in over me; the deep surrounded me; weeds were wrapped around my head at the roots of the mountains. I went down to the land whose bars closed upon me forever; yet you brought up my life from the Pit, O Lord my God. As my life was ebbing away, I remembered the Lord; and my prayer came to you, into your holy temple. Those who worship vain idols *forsake their true loyalty. But I with the voice of thanksgiving will sacrifice to you; what I have vowed I will pay. Deliverance belongs to the Lord!"*

Jonah 2:1–9

The story of Jonah in the belly of a great fish is a powerful example of what happens to our lives when we do not obey the will of God. Often we are blessed with intuitive guidance—the whisper of God directing our path. Yet, we second-guess the wisdom God has given us and pay the price for it, as Jonah did.

The Lord told Jonah to go to Nineveh to protest the wickedness of the people there. Instead of obeying God, Jonah ran away. He hid on board a ship, but when a storm nearly sank the ship, the crew cast him overboard as a sacrifice to the Lord. Jonah paid the price for disregarding the Lord's command by nearly drowning in the raging sea.

The Lord, however, gave Jonah an intriguing second chance by having a large fish swallow him whole, which ironically

gave him shelter for three days and nights. During this time, Jonah realized how badly he had disobeyed God, and he prayed this prayer of praise.

Jonah cried out from the belly of this fish, praising God for not letting him drown and for bringing his life "up from the Pit." We are like Jonah when we realize we have not followed the Lord's divine guidance. We get lost from the path that was set out before us, and we cry out to God to help us find our way back to the path he had given us.

Not only did God answer Jonah's cries of distress, but God also spoke to the fish, and it spewed Jonah out onto dry land. Again, God told Jonah to go to Nineveh. This time, Jonah obeyed.

If there is something in your heart God is telling you to do, don't disobey God and pay the price of being cast out into the open sea of guilt and despair. If we learn to follow God's will the first time around, our lives will be considerably easier in the long run.

Now God be prais'd that to believing souls
Gives light in darkness, comfort in despair!

William Shakespeare, *King Henry VI*

Power Within Us

Now to him who by the power at work within us is able to accomplish abundantly far more than we can ask or imagine, to him be glory in the church and in Christ Jesus to all generations, forever and ever. Amen.

Ephesians 3:20–21

The apostle Paul knew it is God's power within each of us that makes us successful. He understood that when we align ourselves with God's will, we can accomplish far greater things than we had ever imagined. He also knew the glory should always go to God and Christ Jesus.

In Paul's letter to the Ephesians, he created a prayer of gratitude, acknowledgment, and recognition that resonates in our hearts with the truth that we are vessels for God's energy and love. When we come to know that it is not by our own hands that we achieve but by the hands of God guiding us, we realize just how miraculous life can be.

Have you ever struggled to do something that you thought you should do, only to find that no matter what you did or how hard you worked, it simply would not "click"? Perhaps you were not allowing God's mighty power to work in your life. For it is said God does not work for us but through us. Of course, Paul also realized that once God did work a miracle for us, we should be grateful and give glory where glory is due.

Lift up your hearts to Him, sometimes even at your meals, and when you are in company; the least little remembrance will always be acceptable to Him. You need not cry very loud; He is nearer to us than we are aware.

Brother Lawrence

All Who Love Him

Your kingdom is an everlasting kingdom, and your dominion endures throughout all generations.

The Lord is faithful in all his words, and gracious in all his deeds. The Lord upholds all who are falling, and raises up all who are bowed down. The eyes of all look to you, and you give them their food in due season. You open your hand, satisfying the desire of every living thing. The Lord is just in all his ways, and kind in all his doings. The Lord is near to all who call on him, to all who call on him in truth. He fulfills the desire of all who fear him; he also hears their cry, and saves them. The Lord watches over all who love him, but all the wicked he will destroy.

My mouth will speak the praise of the Lord, and all flesh will bless his holy name forever and ever.

Psalm 145:13–21

This psalm is about a great God who is filled with promises for each one of us. He is near all who call on him; he holds up all who are falling; he raises up all who are bowed down; and he watches over all who love him. Truly, he is a God who is faithful and nearby.

The psalmist also reminds us of all God's words and "his doings," the most amazing of which is "satisfying the

desires of every living thing." He is not only a good God and a great God, but he is also a gracious God, one who delights in our delight, and gives us, as the apostle Paul put it, "more than we can ask or imagine" (Eph. 3:20).

This changes our understanding of God, but it also changes us. God fulfills the desires of all who fear him, but he also changes those desires, causing us to speak—and seek—"his holy name forever." We find when we do that, we want entirely different things. And this prayer says we will get them.

Great is thy faithfulness, O God my Father,
There is no shadow of turning with thee;
Thou changest not, thy compassions they fail not;
As thou hast been thou forever will be.
Great is thy faithfulness, great is thy faithfulness,
Morning by morning new mercies I see;
All I have needed thy hand hath provided.
Great is thy faithfulness, Lord unto me.

Thomas O. Chisholm

God Is Everywhere

W Where can I go from your spirit? Or where can I flee from your presence? If I ascend to heaven, you are there; if I make my bed in Sheol, you are there. If I take the wings of the morning and settle at the farthest limits of the sea, even there your hand shall lead me, and your right hand shall hold me fast.

I praise you, for I am fearfully and wonderfully made. Wonderful are your works; that I know very well. My frame was not hidden from you, when I was being made in secret, intricately woven in the depths of the earth. Your eyes beheld my unformed substance. In your book were written all the days that were formed for me, when none of them as yet existed. How weighty to me are your

thoughts, O God! How vast is the sum of them! I try to count them—they are more than the sand; I come to the end—I am still with you.

Psalm 139:7–10, 14–18

God is everywhere. This thought can be either comforting or terrifying. If God is everywhere, he sees us not only when we want him to see us but also when we don't want him to see us. Although the psalmist knew this about God, he found comfort in this truth. Whether God is far above or far below, whether he is far out at sea or deep within the womb, God is still with us, leading us and holding us fast.

The writer finds this comforting because he was "fearfully and wonderfully made" (v. 14). In fact, God had a plan for his entire life: "In your book were written all the days that were formed for me, when none of them as yet existed" (v. 16).

This is a life-changing thought. God knows our end before our beginning. He has a plan for us, and we can have faith that it is a good plan because God himself is good.

Someone is there, I realized. Someone is watching life as it unfolds on this planet. More, Someone is there who loves me. It was a startling feeling of wild hope, a feeling so new and overwhelming that it seemed fully worth risking my life on.

Philip Yancey, *Disappointment with God*

God's Glories

O the depth of the riches and wisdom and knowledge of God! How unsearchable are his judgments and how inscrutable his ways! "For who has known the mind of the Lord? Or who has been his counselor? Or who has given a gift to him, to receive a gift in return?" For from him and through him and to him are all things. To him be the glory forever. Amen.

Romans 11:33–36

Were I a nightingale, I would sing like a nightingale; were I a swan, like a swan. But as it is, I am a rational being, therefore I must sing hymns of praise to God.

Epictetus

In Paul's letter to the beloved of God in Rome, he praised the depths of God's glories in hope that his fellow Christians in Rome would understand that the Lord is all-knowing, all-powerful, and all-giving. Paul compels all of us not to question the judgments and ways of the Lord, for we cannot know his mind.

When we pray to God in faith, trusting that his ways are best, our prayers are always heard, honored, and answered. Remember Paul's words: "from him and through him and to him are all things." God knows our minds, our hearts, our innermost desires, and he gives priceless blessings accordingly.

To glorify God in prayer is to invite his miracles into our lives.

As Christians we want to keep wooing people on God's behalf. We want to tell them the truth about the Lord we love. We want to fan that spark of God's image within them and to explain that the only way to be all they can be is to connect with their Maker.

The Miracles of the Exodus

Then Moses and the Israelites sang this song to the Lord: "I will sing to the Lord, for he has triumphed gloriously; horse and rider he has thrown into the sea. The Lord is my strength and my might, and he has become my salvation; this is my God, and I will praise him, my father's God, and I will exalt him. The Lord is a warrior; the Lord is his name.

"Pharaoh's chariots and his army he cast into the sea; his picked officers were sunk in the Red Sea. The floods covered them; they went down into the depths like a stone. Your right hand, O Lord, glorious in power—your right hand, O Lord, shattered the enemy. In the greatness of your majesty you overthrew your adversaries; you sent out your fury, it consumed them like stubble. At the blast of your nostrils the waters piled up, the floods stood up in a heap; the deeps congealed in the heart of the sea. The enemy said, 'I will pursue, I will overtake, I will divide the spoil, my desire shall have its fill of them. I will draw my sword, my hand shall destroy them.' You blew with your wind, the sea covered them; they sank like lead in the mighty waters.

"Who is like you, O Lord, among the gods? Who is like you, majestic in holiness, awesome in splendor, doing wonders? You stretched out your right hand, the earth swallowed them.

"In your steadfast love you led the people whom you redeemed; you guided them by your strength to your holy abode. The people heard, they trembled; pangs seized the inhabitants of Philistia. Then the chiefs of Edom were dismayed; trembling seized the leaders of Moab; all the inhabitants of Canaan

God, when life feels like a ride that won't let us off, remind us that you are waiting for us to reach up to you. And when we finally do, thank you for being there to lift us to peace and safety. Amen.

melted away. Terror and dread fell upon them; by the might of your arm, they became still as a stone until your people, O Lord, passed by, until the people whom you acquired passed by. You brought them in and planted them on the mountain of your own possession, the place, O Lord, that you made your abode, the sanctuary, O Lord, that your hands have established. The Lord will reign forever and ever."

Exodus 15:1–18

When Moses led the Israelites out of captivity in Egypt, he had the miracle-working power of the Lord as his ally. After God

parted the Red Sea, Moses led the Israelites safely to the other side. Then, while the Egyptian soldiers were in pursuit, God drew the Red Sea together and drowned the soldiers. The hand of God was upon Moses and his people, guiding and protecting them.

Once they reached the opposite shore, Moses and the Israelites sang out in glorious praise and thanks for their salvation and for the steadfast love the Lord had shown them in their greatest moment of need. This prayer, taken from the Book of Exodus, speaks of the depths of their gratitude and reminds us that with God as our ally, we can overcome the forces of evil.

We are told that the Lord performed awesome wonders. "Who is like you, O Lord?" they sang out in awe, for never had they seen such a mighty, majestic God as this. Not only did the Lord guide them safely across the parted sea, but he also provided them with a "mountain of your own possession," a place of sanctuary established with God's own loving hands.

Cave Walkers

We wander like children lost in a cave, perilously close to the edge of despair. Unable to see where we're going, we crouch in fear rather than risk falling while searching for an exit. Nudge us beyond fear; send us guides who have traveled dark passages before.

What does this mean to us today? Each of us has our personal exodus, our journey from pain and suffering to a place of joy and peace, and throughout that journey we can use prayer to call upon God to direct our path. Without the hand of God shielding his people, even Moses could not have protected them. But with God, he was able to lead them out of captivity into the promised land.

If you are being held captive by false beliefs, bad habits, or past resentments, with God's help you, too, can cross the Red Sea of trials and come out safe and secure on the other side. This wonderful prayer proves that there is no

mountain high enough, no ocean deep enough, no valley
wide enough, to keep God from your side.

ll around, the storms may churn,
the seas may rage, the fires burn.
But deep within, you will not fear,
you will have peace when centered there.
For even amidst the tempest wild,
God will be there to guide you, Child.

Barbara Roberts Pine, "All Around, the Storms May Churn"

Praising Nature

O Lord, our Sovereign, how majestic is your name in all the earth!

You have set your glory above the heavens. Out of the mouths of babes and infants you have founded a bulwark because of your foes, to silence the enemy and the avenger.

When I look at your heavens, the work of your fingers, the moon and the stars that you have established; what are human beings that you are mindful of them, mortals that you care for them?

Yet you have made them a little lower than God, and crowned them with glory and honor. You have given them dominion over the works of your hands; you have put all things under their feet, all sheep and oxen, and also the beasts of the field, the birds of the air, and the fish of the sea, whatever passes along the paths of the seas.

O Lord, our Sovereign, how majestic is your name in all the earth!

Psalm 8

Nowhere is God's existence more evident than in the beauty of nature. In this psalm, God's creative presence is glorified in the moon and the stars, as well as in the beasts in the field, the birds in the air, and the fish in the seas.

Psalm 8 prompts us to spend more time appreciating nature, over which the Lord has given us dominion. We have been blessed with a diversity of plants, animals, and gorgeous natural scenery, and it is our responsibility to be good stewards of what God has given us by keeping the earth healthy.

More importantly, the magnificent wonder of the world God has created for us should inspire us to praise him daily for being the marvelous Creator that he is.

*I remember it—
coming from a swim
and lying back in
white sand—
the gift of a moment
to rest,
to sit in reverie,
to watch,
to close eyes and think
of nothing
but the sound of
breaking waves.
Yes, you were there
with the sounds
and the sunshine,
and I am thankful.*

Hannah's Prayer

~~~~~~

Hannah prayed and said, "My heart exults in the Lord; my strength is exalted in my God. My mouth derides my enemies, because I rejoice in my victory.

"There is no Holy One like the Lord, no one besides you; there is no Rock like our God. Talk no more so very proudly, let not arrogance come from your mouth; for the Lord is a God of knowledge, and by him actions are weighed. The bows of the mighty are broken, but the feeble gird on strength. Those who were full have hired themselves out for bread, but those who were hungry are fat with spoil. The barren has borne seven, but she who has many children is forlorn. The Lord kills and brings to life; he brings down to Sheol and raises up. The Lord makes poor and makes rich; he brings low, he also exalts. He raises up the poor from the dust; he lifts the needy from the ash heap, to make them sit with princes and inherit a seat of honor. For the pillars of the earth are the Lord's, and on them he has set the world.

"He will guard the feet of his faithful ones, but the wicked shall be cut off in darkness; for not by might does one prevail. The Lord! His adversaries shall be shattered; the Most High will thunder in heaven. The Lord will judge the ends of the earth; he will give strength to his king, and exalt the power of his anointed."

1 Samuel 2:1–10

The story of Hannah is a story of faith and the power of prayer. Hannah wished for a son, but she was barren. So she bowed to the Lord in silent prayer and supplication, petitioning for a son and promising the Lord that should he answer her prayer, she would give her son to him for his service.

God answered Hannah's prayer in the form of the anointed child, Samuel. In

praise and thanksgiving, she spoke these words and then gave her child into God's service as she had promised. Not only did Samuel grow in stature with his family and community, but also the favor of the Lord was forever upon him.

Hannah knew the Lord had the power to turn her barren body into a fruitful womb. Her faith and belief made her exalted in his sight. She knew that only the Lord could make the poor rich, that only the Lord could raise the dead back to life, and that only the Lord could judge and likewise condemn.

When we pray as Hannah did, we pray with unceasing faith, no matter how impossible our requests might seem. We offer our petition before the Lord with thanks and praise for his might and goodness, knowing that he alone can make the impossible possible.

Even if our dreams and hopes have died, we can delight, knowing if we just put our trust in God, anything can happen.

Great faith is not the faith that walks always in the light and knows no darkness, but the faith that perseveres in spite of God's seeming silences, and the faith that will most certainly and surely get its reward.

Father Andrew

A Glorious Answer

Come Lord Jesus, abide in my heart.

How grateful I am to realize that the answer to my prayer does not depend on me at all. As I quietly abide in you and let your life flow through me, what freedom it is to know that the Father does not see my threadbare patience or insufficient trust, rather only your patience, Lord, and your confidence that the Father has everything in hand.

In your faith I thank you right now for a more glorious answer to my prayer than I can imagine. Amen.

Catherine Marshall, *Adventures in Prayer*

My teenage son often asks me for things that I refuse to give him. It's not that I don't love him, of course, but often he does not see the big picture. There are lessons to be learned and consequences to be avoided that he can't even imagine. The lesson may be as simple as learning to save his own money, and the consequences may be as large as actual, physical harm.

I know, and he knows, that my motive is love and that my wisdom is greater than his. So he usually trusts me, and things work out better than he expected. When it's all over, he usually thanks me.

Prayer is like that, too. The answer God has for our prayer is always better than the one we imagined. So the right response to God should always be "thanks" in the spirit of praise.

Now to him who is able to do immeasurably more than all we ask or imagine, according to his power that is at work within us, to him be glory in the church and in Christ Jesus throughout all generations, for ever and ever! Amen.

Ephesians 3:20–21 NIV

Witnessing Miracles

~

At the time of the offering of the oblation, the prophet Elijah came near and said, "O Lord, God of Abraham, Isaac, and Israel, let it be known this day that you are God in Israel, that I am your servant, and that I have done all these things at your bidding. Answer me, O Lord, answer me, so that this people may know that you, O Lord, are God and that you have turned their hearts back."

1 Kings 18:36–37

The prophet Elijah gathered the Israelites at Mount Carmel, for he had something to show them. He took 12 stones, representing the 12 tribes of Israel (descendants of the sons of Jacob), and built an altar to the Lord. Then he prepared a burnt offering and asked God to demonstrate his mighty power before his people. When God obliged with holy fire that consumed the burnt offering, the people fell on their faces in praise.

When we are on fire with the passion of our love for Christ, it is natural to want to let others witness his miracles for themselves. Elijah did just that on Mount Carmel. We pray that others may know the God we have come to know and that God might turn back the hearts of those who have gone astray.

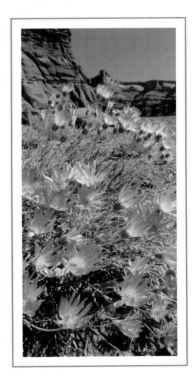

Yet, before we can ask others to serve God, we must acknowledge our own servitude in the same way Elijah did, and we must continually do God's bidding. Then, through the wondrous blessings we experience, others will look upon us and want what we have. And what we have is God.

Lord, give me passion
to care for those who need to know you.
Lord, give me vision
to see what they could become.
Lord, give me ears
to hear what they are really asking.
Lord, give me words
to share my love for you.

Mary's Song of Praise

Mary said, "My soul magnifies the Lord, and my spirit rejoices in God my Savior, for he has looked with favor on the lowliness of his servant. Surely, from now on all generations will call me blessed; for the Mighty One has done great things for me, and holy is his name. His mercy is for those who fear him from generation to generation. He has shown strength with his arm; he has scattered the proud in the thoughts of their hearts. He has brought down the powerful from their thrones, and lifted up the lowly; he has filled the hungry with good things, and sent the rich away empty. He has helped his servant Israel, in remembrance of his mercy, according to the promise he made to our ancestors, to Abraham and to his descendants forever."

Luke 1:46–55

When God chose Mary to be the mother of his Son Jesus, a remarkable miracle was about to occur. It would be an event that would not only change Mary's life but also the life of every person. Mary considered herself a lowly servant to God's will, and the result of her humility was that the Lord exalted her to become the most blessed of women.

When the angel Gabriel first visited Mary and told her of her impending pregnancy, she was stunned, for she was a virgin. Gabriel then addressed her perplexity by explaining that the Holy Spirit would come upon her and that the power of the Most High would overshadow her. In other words, what she herself could not do, God would easily do for her. For with God, all things are possible.

"He . . . has lifted up the lowly; he has filled the hungry with good things," Mary sang with praise, for she was that

Extreme Love

You are everywhere, Lord, and you comfort us while we live through life's extremes. You are with us during births and deaths, in routine and surprise, and in stillness and activity. We cannot wander so far in any direction that you are not already there.

lowly, spiritually hungry person whose soul was overflowing with joy and thanksgiving. No matter what our position in life or what we hunger for, God fills our needs. The blessings of the Lord are not reserved for the rich, the powerful, or the beautiful, but for everyone, no matter how small and insignificant we might think we are.

The exciting message of Mary's song is that our own lives can change at any moment, that a miracle can occur at any time, and that even those of us who consider ourselves lowly and unworthy can receive the most magnificent blessings imaginable when the Lord is active in our lives. In many

ways, we are all like Mary, willing to give birth at any time to the wondrous plan the Lord has intended for each of us.

Known as "The Canticle of Mary," the Magnificat, Mary's song of praise, has become a crucial part of the liturgy of the church since the fourth century. This beautiful prayer of joy and thanksgiving comes from the Gospel of Luke. Mary, pregnant with Jesus, was visiting her cousin Elizabeth, who was pregnant with John the Baptist at the time. At this special visit between the two blessed and holy women, Elizabeth greeted Mary with the well-known phrase: "Blessed art thou among women, blessed is the fruit of thy womb," which later became part of the prayer, "Hail Mary." The canticle was Mary's response to this greeting.

Lifelong Refuge

〜

You, O Lord, are my hope, my trust, O Lord, from my youth. Upon you I have leaned from my birth; it was you who took me from my mother's womb. My praise is continually of you.

I have been like a portent to many, but you are my strong refuge. My mouth is filled with your praise, and with your glory all day long. Do not cast me off in the time of old age; do not forsake me when my strength is spent.

Psalm 71:5–9

My parents recently celebrated their fiftieth anniversary. We had a big party on the beach near Sarasota, Florida, in a restaurant overlooking the gulf, where the sun sinks each night in a sea of purple and pink.

Everyone who rose to congratulate them commented on the same remarkable thing—their life of faith and their faithfulness to God. It was a magical and memorable moment—a moment filled with laughter and tears.

Although Mom has suffered a stroke and Dad has had to limit his own goals to care for her, they have praised God and found refuge in him. Both are quite confident that God will not "cast them off in the time of old age."

The result is a joy that transforms their journey, even as it ends. They have a view of a greater gulf, a view where the light of heaven pales the multicolored glory of the setting sun.

The righteous will flourish like a palm tree, they will grow like a cedar of Lebanon; planted in the house of the Lord, they will flourish in the courts of our God. They will still bear fruit in old age, they will stay fresh and green, proclaiming, "The Lord is upright; he is my Rock, and there is no wickedness in him."

Psalm 92:12–15 NIV

From Distress to Joy

For his anger is but for a moment; his favor is for a lifetime. Weeping may linger for the night, but joy comes with the morning.

As for me, I said in my prosperity, "I shall never be moved." By your favor, O Lord, you had established me as a strong mountain; you hid your face; I was dismayed.

To you, O Lord, I cried, and to the Lord I made supplication: "What profit is there in my death, if I go down to the Pit? Will the dust praise you? Will it tell of your faithfulness? Hear, O Lord, and be gracious to me! O Lord, be my helper!"

You have turned my mourning into dancing; you have taken off my sackcloth and clothed me with joy, so that my soul may praise you and not be silent. O Lord my God, I will give thanks to you forever.

Psalm 30:5–12

I was raised in a conservative tradition where we were not allowed to dance. Sometimes I think this is unfortunate because I don't know what to do when I experience the joy of the Lord.

The psalmist did, however. He danced, expressing with body and soul the joy of God's presence in his life. At the time, he had been in deep distress, having lost something he cared deeply for. He was so discouraged that he even despaired of his life. It was then that the Lord reached down and turned his mourning into dancing.

My flesh and my heart may fail, but God is the strength of my heart and my portion forever.

Psalm 73:26

> *The Lord is my strength and my shield; in him my heart trusts; so I am helped, and my heart exults, and with my song I give thanks to him.*
>
> Psalm 28:7

I never learned to dance, but I have learned to grieve. About 12 years ago, when our two-year-old son was in intensive care for two weeks, clinging to life after choking on a carrot and going into severe respiratory distress, just the possibility of losing him overwhelmed me. At the same time, I was angry at God for letting it happen, and I was angry with my own dad, who lived on the other side of the country, for not coming to be with me. Every day I would talk to him on the phone, and he would ask if he should come. Everyday I would say no. More than anything, it seemed, I wanted him to come without me asking.

Finally, I asked, and he came. The moment he walked into the waiting room was one of the most intense moments of joy in my life. My son recovered, and so did my faith—both in my dad and in my God. It almost made me dance.

I think this was the psalmist's experience. He was in great distress, but when he asked his heavenly Father to come, he did. And God turned his mourning into praise and clothed him with joy.

Joy to the world! the Lord is come;
Let earth receive her king;
Let every heart prepare him room
And heaven and nature sing.
Joy to the earth! The Savior reigns;
Let men their songs employ;
While fields and floods, rocks, hills and plains
Repeat the sounding joy.

Issac Watts, "Joy to the World"

A New Birth

Blessed be the God and Father of our Lord Jesus Christ! By his great mercy he has given us a new birth into a living hope through the resurrection of Jesus Christ from the dead, and into an inheritance that is imperishable, undefiled, and unfading, kept in heaven for you, who are being protected by the power of God through faith for a salvation ready to be revealed in the last time.

1 Peter 1:3–5

As we trust in the perfect love of God, we can let go of the worries and fears that hold us captive. "Cast all your anxiety on him," said Peter, "because he cares for you."

1 Peter 5:7

The apostle Peter's prayer of praise and hope was part of a letter meant for the Jewish exiles of the Dispersion. These chosen people whom God had called upon were residing as aliens throughout Pontius, Galatia, Cappadocia, Asia, and Bithynia. These people had become believers in Christ and, as Peter stated, had been "sprinkled" with the blood of the Lord and the promise of salvation. Nevertheless, they were living as outcasts with trials and tribulations to overcome. Peter consoled them by telling them that they would receive entrance into heaven through their faith in Jesus, whom Peter knew intimately.

Even for those of us not in physical exile, this prayer promises us a new birth that will bring us into a divine inheritance that cannot be taken from us. We can use this prayer as a vehicle of faith that will prepare us for a life everlasting in the "last time," as Peter refers to, where we will spend our days seated at the Lord's table in heaven.

A Safe Place

So many terrors and troubles confront us, so many dangers and calamities. Is anyone ever completely safe? Only when we trust God do we know peace and assurance in the shelter of his care.

A King's Testimony

O magnify the Lord with me, and let us exalt his name together. I sought the Lord, and he answered me, and delivered me from all my fears. Look to him, and be radiant; so your faces shall never be ashamed. This poor soul cried, and was heard by the Lord, and was saved from every trouble. The angel of the Lord encamps around those who fear him, and delivers them. O taste and see that the Lord is good; happy are those who take refuge in him.

Psalm 34:3–8

King David, the greatest king of ancient Israel, wrote many of the psalms in the Bible. This one has 22 verses in all, which make up what is known as an "alphabetical psalm." This means that the letters that begin each verse in its original language make up the Hebrew alphabet.

Here is a king's testimony to answered prayer. David had offered a prayer for help, and God answered, delivering him from his enemies. It makes sense that he would speak of his "poor soul crying out," because these words were written to commemorate an event in David's life that was extremely perilous—his escape from a foreign king's prison.

How did David do it? Traditional inscriptions above this psalm usually say something along these lines: "Of David, when he pretended madness before Abimelech the king, who drove him away, and he departed." So, by a form of subterfuge, David escaped. And he lived to thank God for his life!

When God delivers us from troubles, we naturally want to thank and praise him. Will you, too, look to him with

a radiant, unashamed face? You will if, like David, you have tasted and found that God is good and merciful.

Who was my sorrow for
last week when from my mud-room door
I watched an arrogant mallard drake,
From a wintering-over flock of eight,
Fly to my lawn from a nearby lake.
He stumbled, injured,
Right leg strong, left folding down.
I watched that green-headed, curly-tailed drake
Hesitate. Then, heeding a hen's loud call,
He hobbled to corn scattered near a garden wall.
Oh, God, I am injured, too
My sorrows slow to mend.
But today, as I turned from the mud-room door
Came the call of a faithful friend.

The Sacrifice of Praise

Quicken me with a spirit of praise, dear Lord. May my mouth be filled with praises for you today.

Joni Eareckson Tada, *More Precious Than Silver*

A diving accident in 1967 left Joni Eareckson Tada a quadriplegic in a wheelchair, unable to use her hands. During two years of rehabilitation, she spent long months learning how to paint with a brush between her teeth.

While that would leave most of us utterly demoralized, Joni turned her disability into a ceaseless symphony of praise. She is the author of 27 best-selling and award-winning devotional books. She is also an outspoken advocate for people with disabilities.

Her positive, cheerful message reminds all of us to make the ultimate sacrifice—the sacrifice of praise.

Through him, then, let us continually offer a sacrifice of praise to God, that is, the fruit of lips that confess his name.

Hebrews 13:15

Clothed in Light

～∾～

Bless the Lord, O my soul. O Lord my God, you are very great. You are clothed with honor and majesty, wrapped in light as with a garment. You stretch out the heavens like a tent, you set the beams of your chambers on the waters, you make the clouds your chariot, you ride on the wings of the wind, you make the winds your messengers, fire and flame your ministers.

Psalm 104:1–4

Our God is a big God. He rides the clouds and sets the foundation of his dwelling on the sea. Even more remarkable are his clothes. The Lord is clothed in majesty and light. We can't comprehend majesty, so it is the "light" that fascinates us, partly because we know what light looks like and partly because we know what it does.

Light helps us see the paths we should take. More importantly, it dispels the darkness, helping us see danger, as well as opportunity. This is good because we are often blinded to that which is pure and true and lovely.

Sun of our life, thy
quickening ray
Sheds on our path the
glow of day;
Star of our hope, thy
softened light
Cheers the long
watches of the night.

Oliver Wendell Holmes,
"Lord of All Being,
Throned Afar"

Praise God that his light extends everywhere. Fire and flame are his ministers, and his light both helps me see and keeps me warm.

That Thou, O God my life has lighted,
With ray of light, steady, ineffable, vouchsafed of Thee,
Light rare untellable, lighting the very light,
Beyond all signs, descriptions, languages:
For that O God, be it my latest word, here on my knees,
Old, poor and paralyzed, I thank Thee.

Walt Whitman, *Prayers of Columbus*

Pray for God's Blessings

*Glory to thee, my God, this night
for all the blessings of the light.*

Thomas Ken

God's Perfect Plan

Father, once—it seems very long ago now—I had such big dreams, so much anticipation of the future. Now no shimmering horizon beckons me.

Where is your plan for my life, Father?

You have told us that without a vision, we perish. So Father in heaven, knowing that I can ask in confidence for what is your expressed will to give me, I ask you to deposit in my mind and heart the particular dream, the special vision you have for my life.

And along with the dream, will you give me whatever graces, patience, and stamina it takes to see the dream through? This may involve adventures I have not bargained for. But I want to trust you enough to follow, even if you lead along new paths.

Lord, if you have to break down any prisons of mine before I can see the stars and catch the vision, then Lord, begin the process now. In joyous expectation. Amen.

Catherine Marshall, *Adventures in Prayer*

The Lord once told the prophet Jeremiah, "For surely I know the plans I have for you, says the Lord, plans for your welfare and not for harm, to give you a future with hope. Then when you call upon me and come and pray to me, I will hear you" (Jer. 29:11–12). It is evident from these words that our best interests are close to God's heart and that prayer can keep our dreams alive—once we are willing to trust God to make them come true.

This should be easy to do, but, like Catherine Marshall, we often lose sight of some great promise or vision, discouraged by the pressure of circumstances. In such spiritual despair, we can ask the Lord for a fresh vision and for the strength to achieve that vision.

Wait in "joyous expectation" for God's great blessings to begin in your life.

This is what the Sovereign Lord says: "The days are near when every vision will be fulfilled."

Ezekiel 12:23 NIV

The Wisdom of Solomon

Solomon said, "You have shown great and steadfast love to your servant my father David, because he walked before you in faithfulness, in righteousness, and in uprightness of heart toward you; and you have kept for him this great and steadfast love, and have given him a son to sit on his throne today. And now, O Lord my God, you have made your servant king in place of my father David, although I am only

a little child; I do not know how to go out or come in. And your servant is in the midst of the people whom you have chosen, a great people, so numerous they cannot be numbered or counted. Give your servant therefore an understanding mind to govern your people, able to discern between good and evil; for who can govern this your great people?"

1 Kings 3:6–9

In the first Book of Kings, we learn that Solomon dearly loved the Lord when he was young and first became king of Israel. This particular prayer was Solomon's answer to the Lord when the Lord appeared to him in a dream and said, "Ask what I should give you?" (v. 5).

Solomon could have asked for anything, and the Lord would no doubt have obliged him. Because Solomon did not ask for material riches, long life, or revenge against his enemies, however, the Lord blessed Solomon with what he truly desired—the gift of wisdom and discernment. In fact, the Lord

Some people say, "When all else fails, pray," but wise folks never wait that long.

made Solomon wiser than all who came before him and all who would come after him.

Jesus often told his followers to first seek God's kingdom and not ask for specific material things. If we do this, he told us, we would also be given everything else we need. Indeed, if we seek God above all other things, we end up with more than we could ever have hoped for.

Solomon became a king among kings because of his newfound wisdom, and we, too, can become exalted when we learn to discern the voice of God within us. For true happiness and success in all areas of life come from following the voice of the Lord, who is always urging us to walk in his ways, for his ways are always the highest and the best.

It's clear that our path to heaven is a delightful one. Our lives are to be holy because of our connection with Christ, and our lives are also to be whole, complete, and packed to overflowing with the good things God gives to us.

Bless You and Keep You

The Lord bless you and keep you; the Lord make his face to shine upon you, and be gracious to you; the Lord lift up his countenance upon you, and give you peace.

Numbers 6:24–26

The Lord gave this prayerlike benediction through Moses to Aaron and his sons as a way to greet the ancient Israelites. It was the Lord's way of blessing and showing his delight in his people.

Throughout history, this wonderful prayer has been exchanged as a gift of blessings between friends and strangers alike. It is a way to acknowledge one another and wish one another the good graces and abiding peace that only the Lord can bestow upon his beloved children.

Bless my neighbors, Lord, through my smiles, in my encouraging words, and by my helping hand.

Jabez's Prayer

Jabez called on the God of Israel, saying, "Oh, that you would bless me and enlarge my border, and that your hand might be with me, and that you would keep me from hurt and harm!" And God granted what he asked.

1 Chronicles 4:10

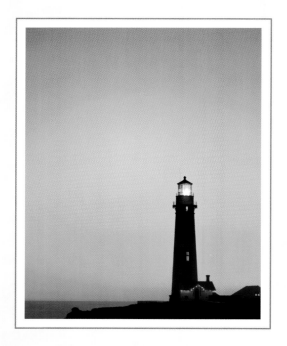

Jabez was one of many brothers who belonged to the tribe of Judah, one of the 12 tribes of Israel. Although he was born in pain, his mother favored him, naming him Jabez (see 1 Chron. 4:9). This otherwise obscure biblical character is well known because of a best-selling book that bears his name and focuses on the simple prayer he offered to the God of Israel.

Jabez asked God for a special blessing. He wanted God's hand to guide him and protect him from all harm, but most interestingly, he wanted God to "enlarge" his land. Jabez desired what we all desire—to have an abundant life blessed with increase and expansion, whether it be better finances, more success, more offspring, or more opportunities.

Because so little is said about this man, Jabez's words are open to interpretation. The final sentence, however, is clear. "And God granted what he asked." This simple two-sentence verse gives us faith and assurance that our prayers are not only acknowledged but also answered.

Jesus told us to ask for what we wanted and that the power of our belief and faith would allow us to receive what we asked for. Jabez's prayer reminds us that no matter how obscure we may sometimes feel, God still hears us and answers our prayers.

There is not in this world a kind of life more sweet and delightful than that of a continual walk with God.

Brother Lawrence

Glimpses of God

You whom I glimpse perhaps
In the motion of a thought
and the uplift of my spirit?
You I have never seen,
Yet in you I believe and hope.

Francois Chagneau

The French countryside is filled with nearly a hundred abbeys and monasteries, many of them built of stones that have endured for centuries. In the heart of the forest of Boquen

stands one of the most simple yet beautiful of these buildings. It is considered a "high place of meditation," and its history goes back to A.D. 1137 when Cistercian monks established it. They remained there until the French Revolution when the abbey was plundered and fell into disrepair.

In 1936, the antique abbey was rebuilt, stone by stone, rising out of its ruins not only as a building but once again as a center of monastic life, which remains vibrant to this day. Today it shelters the Sisters of Bethlehem, who, in keeping with their vows of solitude, devote their lives to serving God and humankind.

One of the lay members of the Boquen Abbey, François Chagneau, wrote the lines that form a portion of the larger prayer entitled: "Who Are You, My God?" He continues to write prayers for the community at Boquen, prayers that are

The blessings of the Lord are priceless and are to be cherished above all else.

You are everywhere, Lord, and we're comforted to be enfolded as we move through life's extremes. You are with us in birthings and dyings, in routine and surprise, and in stillness and activity. We cannot wander so far in any direction that you are not already there.

known for their depth of honesty and sense of longing for a closer walk with God. In this prayer Chagreau asks the question that fills every heart seeking greater understanding: *Who, exactly, are You? And where can You truly be found?*

It is a quality of the spiritual journey that we, who are finite, can attain only glimpses of the infinite shining through our everyday experiences. This is the glory of our God, that being Spirit, he is nevertheless revealed to us in the ordinary things of life. Chagreau speaks of the horizon, the earth, the sea, and even his own thoughts as conveyors of the reality and presence of God.

Are these enough to keep us believing? Though we cannot see the wind, we see its effects. Though we cannot

fully "explain" the sunlight, we are warmed by its presence. Although God remains invisible, yet we believe and hope in him; we have experienced him, especially in our most trying moments.

What can be a better blessing from God than knowing God himself? To finally arrive at a firm belief in this unseen reality, which is infinite love, is to have our lives changed forever.

In our finiteness, we must continually drop to our faces before God in worship, saying, I bow before You as one of Your creatures. Thank You that, while I cannot understand everything, my hand is held by the eternal, all-wise, Infinite God, the Creator.

Edith Schaeffer, *Affliction*

In God's House

For a day in your courts is better than a thousand elsewhere. I would rather be a doorkeeper in the house of my God than live in the tents of wickedness. For the Lord God is a sun and shield; he bestows favor and honor. No good thing does the Lord withhold from those who walk uprightly. O Lord of hosts, happy is everyone who trusts in you.

Psalm 84:10–12

We took sweet counsel together, and walked unto the house of God in company.

Psalm 55:14 KJV

Madeline goes to our church. She is 85, but she still plays the organ sometimes when our regular musician is away. It is my privilege just about every week to hold the door for her at the end of the service. Sometimes, if I'm lucky, I get a warm hug from her.

I think I know what the psalmist is talking about when he says he would rather be a doorkeeper in the house of God than do just about anything else. Loving people is the sacred work of porters and ushers who, week after week, hold the doors of God's house. Helping people find a seat is not a highly glamorous job, of course, but it is in a glamorous place—the house of God. And the rewards are great.

There is no place like it, a place where blessing abounds: "No good thing does the Lord withhold from those who walk uprightly," the psalmist says.

No wonder it's a job blessed with many joys.

These things I remember as I pour out my soul: how I used to go with the multitude, leading the procession to the house of God, with shouts of joy and thanksgiving among the festive throng.

Psalm 42:4 NIV

Reign in Thy Glory

Grant, O Lord, that we may live in thy fear, die in thy favour, rest in thy peace, rise in thy power, reign in thy glory.

William Laud

You and I do not have a thing to fear simply because we are growing older. If our faith is firmly fixed in the Savior, we can count on Him to be waiting at the end of the road to greet us. . . . He will welcome us home.

Charles Swindoll,
Living on the Ragged Edge

Some of the views of English Archbishop William Laud triggered a reaction from Puritans who eventually sailed the Atlantic. Thus 20 towns and 16,000 Americans quickly came into existence because of him. Still, there was no reason why any Puritan might not properly pray Laud's prayer.

For any of us, contemplating life's ending can be a life-changing exercise. We'll be reminded to live in the reverence of God while we're on this earth. Having lived close to God here, we will enjoy the blessings of our reign with him in heaven.

Steadfast Love

How precious is your steadfast love, O God! All people may take refuge in the shadow of your wings. They feast on the abundance of your house, and you give them drink from the river of your delights. For with you is the fountain of life; in your light we see light.

O continue your steadfast love to those who know you, and your salvation to the upright of heart!

Psalm 36:7–10

In this psalm, King David is declaring the awesomeness of God's love. It is a blessing that he delights in, and his prayer is that the Lord will continue to send this priceless blessing his way.

In our culture today, love is a thing that seems to come and go. We fall into it and, just as quickly, fall out again. Not so with God! His love is reliable, unwavering, ongoing, unstoppable, and life changing. In his steadfastness, he will be there for you. Always.

I can speak to you through prayer; your own Holy Spirit responds. Yet one thing more I must have truly to be one with you. And that is love.

Marjorie Holmes,
How Can I Find You, God?

A Soldier's Prayer

I asked God for strength, that I might achieve.
I was made weak, that I might learn humbly to obey.
I asked for health, that I might do greater things.
I was given infirmity, that I might do better things.
I asked for riches, that I might be happy.
I was given poverty, that I might be wise.
I asked for power, that I might have the praise of men.
I was given weakness, that I might feel the need of God.
I asked for all things, that I might enjoy life.
I was given life, that I might enjoy all things.
I got nothing that I asked for—but everything that
    I had hoped for.
Almost despite myself, my unspoken prayers were
    answered.
I am among all men, most richly blessed.

Author Unknown

This "Prayer of an Unknown Confederate Soldier" is said to have been part of a letter found on the body of a Confederate soldier killed in the line of duty. We may never know his identity, but his words live on in this powerful prayer of the grace of God's will.

This soldier prayed for many things. He asked for strength, for health, for riches, for power, for all the typical things a man desires. Instead, God gave him even greater blessings by *not* answering his prayers. God chose to give him weakness, infirmity, and poverty, and the end result was that all the desires of the soldier's heart were answered in a way he never could have imagined. He, indeed, received nothing he asked for but everything he needed.

How easy it is for us to try to tell God not only what miracle we want in our lives but also exactly how he should accomplish it. Yet, our Creator has his own purposes, not the least of which is to teach us that he is in control—not us.

This empowering prayer joyfully proves that God knows best what we need and that his vision for us always outshines our own limited vision for ourselves. The Unknown Soldier may not have been healthy, rich, or powerful, as he had hoped, but he was made wise, humble, and prosperous in the important things worth having—the joys of life itself. He learned what Jesus taught his disciples—to seek God's kingdom first and all else will be given to you as a result.

Have you ever prayed for something, only to later feel relieved and grateful that God had not given you what you desired? That, in fact, God had brought you something far greater then what your limited mind could conceive? This is what the "Prayer of an Unknown Confederate Soldier" is about: the wonderful fact that God truly knows what we want and need, even when we are not sure of it ourselves.

"Almost despite myself," the soldier writes, "my unspoiled prayers were answered." We can remember this the next time our prayers are not answered or are answered in such a way that makes us question God's intentions.

God moves in a mysterious way,
His wonders to perform.
He plants his footsteps in the sea
And rides upon the storm.

William Cowper,
"Light Shining Out of Darkness"

Perhaps, almost despite ourselves, when we pray from our hearts, we will get not what we wanted but what God wants us to have.

Thou, who hast trod the thorny road,
Wilt share each small distress;
The love which bore the greater load
Will not refuse the less.
There is no secret sigh we breathe
But meets Thine ear divine;
And every cross grows light beneath,
The shadow, Lord, of Thine.

Jane Drewdson, "There Is No Sorrow, Lord, Too Light"

We Ask Thee

But we ask Thee for Thy holy privilege. We know we can do nothing without Thy aid or assistance. We ask Thee, give us the spirit of Christ and determination to press onward and upward. We ask Thee to give us, Father, grace, hope, patience, and keep our feet in the straight and narrow path and ever to be willing to do the task Thou hast assigned to us.

Sunday School Prayers, 1933

This is the confidence we have in approaching God: that if we ask anything according to his will, he hears us.

1 John 5:14 NIV

This is one of dozens of prayers found in a group of steno-graphic reports of African American Sunday School worship services published in 1933.

A close reading shows they are exactly right. In this short prayer they acknowledge their need: "We can do nothing without thy aid." And they ask for help three times: "We ask thee...."

It's a good way to start Sunday school—or any day of your week.

The Lord Challenges Job

~

Then Job arose, tore his robe, shaved his head, and fell on the ground and worshiped. He said, "Naked I came from my mother's womb, and naked shall I return there; the Lord gave, and the Lord has taken away; blessed be the name of the Lord."

Job 1:20–21

The story of Job is about a man whose faith in God was challenged to the utmost. Yet, no matter what was taken from him and no matter how much he suffered, Job did not blame God for his sorrows and physical afflictions. He did lose hope at times. He did doubt and question. He did whine and complain. After all, his suffering was horrendous. But through it all, he did not turn away from God.

When we realize that the Lord has the power to give and to take, we understand that the Lord allows things to happen—even difficult and painful things. To humble ourselves before God's power even when we want to yell at God is to

show the kind of faith and integrity that Job had. We may stumble and turn away from God temporarily, but if we look within our deepest hearts, we will know that we are being molded and disciplined in the mysterious ways of the Lord. And if we hold fast to God, our reward will be twofold, as it was for Job.

Lord, when it hurts too much to even pray, when pain overwhelms us, you are still here, close and caring.

You cannot control every circumstance, but you can respond to each one in faith.

Ellis Morrison, *Life Hurts—God Heals!*

A Bedtime Hymn

Glory to thee, my God, this night
for all the blessings of the light;
keep me, O keep me, King of kings,
Beneath thy own almighty wings.
Forgive me, Lord, for thy dear Son,
The ill that I this day have done,
That with the world, myself, and thee
I, ere I sleep, at peace may be.

Thomas Ken

Let me meditate upon the dark nights through which I have come, the sinister things from which I have been delivered and have a grateful heart.

Peter Marshall,
The Prayers of Peter Marshall

There is a sweet irony between the words of this hymn prayer that asks a peaceful night of sleep and the venue in which it was often originally sung. Imagine a group of young men at Winchester College in England passionately singing these words of prayer before retiring, sometimes with raucous, jubilant voices.

Interestingly, tourists to the college can still see, carved into stone, the name of one of those teenage students: T. Ken, who later became the author of this hymn. Years later, Ken served as chaplain to King Charles II.

Whether uttered in quiet solitude or as a joyful exercise in group singing, this prayer is life changing if we let it move us into more peacefulness as bedtime approaches and as we consider all the blessings God has showered upon us. After all, what can be better than to lay our heads down and know that we are at peace with the world, ourselves, and God?

The day has been long, Lord, but that's water under the bridge. Bless me now with stillness and sleep. I sigh and turn over, knowing that night will usher in the day with new joys and possibilities, blessings from your ever-wakeful Spirit.

The Center of Faith

~∾~

O give thanks to the Lord, for he is good; his stead-fast love endures forever!

Let Israel say, "His steadfast love endures forever." Let the house of Aaron say, "His steadfast love endures forever." Let those who fear the Lord say, "His steadfast love endures forever."

Out of my distress I called on the Lord; the Lord answered me and set me in a broad place. With the Lord on my side I do not fear. What can mortals do to me? The Lord is on my side to help me; I shall look in triumph on those who hate me. It is better to take refuge in the Lord than to put confidence in mortals. It is better to take refuge in the Lord than to put confidence in princes.

Psalm 118:1–9

This is an interesting text, perhaps made more interesting by the fact that it is exactly in the center of the Bible. If you count the verses in front of it and the verses behind it, you will find that at the exact numerical center of the Scriptures it says, "It is better to take refuge in the Lord than to put confidence in mortals" (v. 8).

This is also the exact center of what the Scriptures teach us: That we must put our faith in God instead of people. He is the Creator and our heavenly Father. Jesus said the first and greatest commandment was that we should love the Father with all of our heart. Everything the Bible teaches begins and ends with this commandment.

Obviously, the way we love God is by trusting him, especially in view of how this particular prayer begins. We are told four times that "his steadfast love endures forever." And then we are told, twice, that he is on our side.

The works of his hands are faithful and just; all his precepts are trustworthy. They are steadfast for ever and ever, done in faithfulness and uprightness. He provided redemption for his people; he ordained his covenant forever— holy and awesome is his name.

Psalm 111:7–9 NIV

The Protestant Reformer Martin Luther related this truth in one of his hymns: "A mighty fortress is our God, a bulwark never failing." It is a truth that caused the ancient Hebrew king who wrote this prayer to also say, "Some take pride in chariots, and some in horses, but our pride is in the name of the Lord our God" (Ps. 20:7). The missionary pioneer Hudson Taylor knew it, too, and on his death bed, he said, "I can only lie still in God's arms like a little child, and trust him."

A steadfast God with steadfast love. What's not to trust? No wonder it is better to take refuge in the Lord than to put our confidence in others. It is a truth that rightly belongs at the center of our faith and our lives.

Love divine, all loves excelling,
Joy of heaven, to earth come down,
Fix in us thy humble dwelling;
All thy faithful mercies crown.
Jesus thou art all compassion,
Pure, unbounded love thou art;
Visit us with thy salvation;
Enter every trembling heart.
Finish then thy new creation;
Pure and spotless let us be;
Let us see thy great salvation,
Perfectly restored in thee.
Changed from glory into glory,
Till in heaven we take our place,
Till we cast our crowns before thee,
Lost in wonder, love, and praise.

For you have been my hope, O Sovereign Lord, my confidence since my youth.

Psalm 71:5 NIV

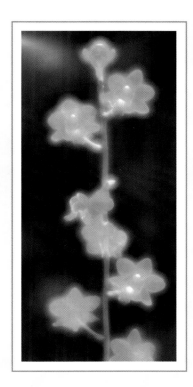

The Lord's Medicine

Lord Jesus, you are medicine to me when I am sick, strength to me when I need help, life itself when I fear death, the way when I long for heaven, the light when all is dark, and food when I need nourishment. Glory be to you forever. Amen.

St. Ambrose

Ambrose was a bishop in Milan in the fourth century. He became the Patron Saint of Learning. Ambrose committed his life to Christ while writing many beautiful prayers that praised the Lord for all of his blessings—good and wonderful.

To Ambrose, Christ's presence was like medicine to a sick person, strength to a weak person, life to a person near death, light in the darkness, and food for a mal-nourished spirit. We, too, can live in the presence of the Lord and be healed, be empowered, and be given food for our hungry souls and everlasting life if we walk in the ways of the Lord.

By praising God, we open ourselves to God. By showing our love for God, we receive more of his love in return. By giving God the glory he deserves, we are given more glorious blessings in return. In other words, we have nothing to fear, and we lack for nothing when we give ourselves to the Lord.

We can rest in peaceful assurance that we will be cared for and protected, loved and guided. That is why Ambrose calls Christ "Our Comforting Lord."

Sheep of God's Pasture

Despite today's valley of shadow and sickness, shepherd of my soul, I know you will restore me to the safe meadow of wellness.

Hail Mary

~≈~

Hail Mary, full of grace. The Lord is with thee. Blessed art thou amongst women, and blessed is the fruit of thy womb, Jesus.

Holy Mary, Mother of God, pray for us sinners, now and at the hour of our death.

Amen.

The "Hail Mary" prayer is the most familiar of all prayers used by the Roman Catholic Church to honor the mother of

Jesus. It is also referred to as the "Angelical Salutation" because the first words in its Latin form are "Ave Maria." This devotion to Mary is both a petition for her graces and a prayer of thanksgiving for her blessed fruit, Christ himself.

Though it is a Roman Catholic invocation, its words can speak to all Christians of the power of a mother's love for her son and of the love only a mother can give to those in need. Throughout history, it has been almost as well known as the "Lord's Prayer" and the "Apostle's Creed." Commonly associated with angels, this prayer was often inscribed on bells during the eleventh and twelfth centuries.

Those who pray the "Hail Mary" ask for special gifts and good graces from the mother of Christ. She stands above all women, and she is exceedingly holy. Therefore, we turn to her for help even in our darkest hours. Because of these words

In silence
I kneel in your
presence—
bowing my heart
to your wisdom;
lifting my hands
for your mercy;
and opening my soul to
your great gift.
I am already held
in your arms.

of mercy, particularly said at the hour of death, this inspiring prayer provides many Christians throughout the world with tremendous comfort and peace.

To pray the "Hail Mary" is also to recognize the impor-

tance of both asking for help and giving praise to the woman chosen to give birth to the Son of God. We honor Mary for her unique place in God's plan. Once we have given her our reverence, we then ask her to pray for us, knowing that her attention to our suffering will not go unheeded. No matter what our sins, the mother of our Lord prays for us. No matter what our troubles, she hears us. No matter what our sufferings, she consoles us.

"Holy Mary, Mother of God!" Who is more deserving

of our thanks and our devotion than the woman who nurtured Jesus to become the man, teacher, and leader that he was? Mary, to whom so many people have turned during their times of need, can help us become the Christians we so long to be.

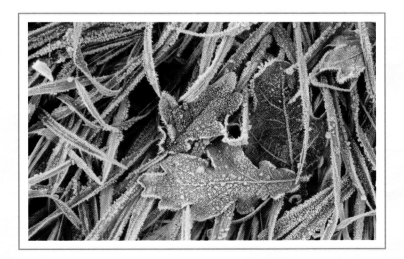

The "Hail Mary" prayer consists of three distinct parts. The first, "Hail Mary, full of grace, the Lord is with thee, blessed art thou amongst women," embodies words spoken by the angel Gabriel as a salutation to the Blessed Mother (Luke 1:28). The second part, "and blessed is the fruit of thy womb, Jesus," was inspired by the greeting of St. Elizabeth upon meeting Mary (v. 42). The final part, or the actual petition, "Holy Mary, Mother of God, pray for us sinners now and at the hour of our death," was added by the official Catechism of the Council of Trent as a way for sinners to reconcile themselves with God and obtain blessings in the present life and for all eternity.

Extol Our Lord!

I will extol you, my God and King, and bless your name forever and ever. Every day I will bless you, and praise your name forever and ever. Great is the Lord, and greatly to be praised; his greatness is unsearchable. One generation shall laud your works to another, and shall declare your mighty acts.

Psalm 145:1–4

The psalmist invites us to live in the light of God's goodness and greatness. To extol him is to tell him these things: "You are an awesome God; you are the greatest." If we neglect this opportunity to praise and bless God, we will miss out on the marvelous blessing of acknowledging the King of the Universe and how wonderful his mighty deeds are.

Having an attitude of praise has tremendous life-changing potential. The challenge is simply to look up more than we look down. It's easy to become focused on all of life's "downers"—irritations, frustrations, losses, and disappointments. Yet, when we take a moment to look up and become aware of God's presence, our perspective radically changes. For example, when we appreciate the fresh air we're breathing, feel the warmth of the sun shin-

ing down on our shoulders, or enjoy the moonglow in a friend's face, we are reminded of how God has blessed us on this earth. Therefore, we extol our Lord.

When once I had seen the great beauty of the Lord, I saw no one by comparison on whom my thoughts wished to dwell.

Teresa of Avila

Our Shield

To you, O Lord, I call; my rock, do not refuse to hear me, for if you are silent to me, I shall be like those who go down to the Pit. Hear the voice of my supplication, as I cry to you for help, as I lift up my hands toward your most holy sanctuary. Do not drag me away with the wicked, with those who are workers of evil, who speak peace with their neighbors, while mischief is in their hearts. . . .

Blessed be the Lord, for he has heard the sound of my pleadings. The Lord is my strength and my shield; in him my heart trusts; so I am helped, and my heart exults, and with my song I give thanks to him.

The Lord is the strength of his people; he is the saving refuge of his anointed. O save your people, and bless your heritage; be their shepherd, and carry them forever.

Psalm 28:1–3, 6–9

After Abraham rescued his nephew Lot from the four kings of the plains, the king of Sodom offered to let him keep all the spoils of war. This seems like a strange offer since Abraham had won the battle outright and was entitled to everything anyway. Rather than let it appear, however, that the king of Sodom was the source of his wealth, Abraham turned it all down.

Almost immediately, the Lord appeared to Abraham and said, "Do not be afraid, I am your shield and your very great reward." The Lord himself was Abraham's protection and provision. He didn't say he was *like* a shield. He said he *was* the shield. And he himself was the reward.

This is a comforting story, and this is a comforting prayer, for it teaches us that we have all we need in the Lord. In fact, the psalmist praises the Lord for being our rock, our strength, our shield, our refuge, and our shepherd. In other places in the Bible, God is said to be our tower, our fortress, our bread, our water, our path, and our light.

That's a lot. And that's certainly enough.

O worship the king, all glorious above;
O gratefully sing his power and his love;
Our Shield and Defender, the Ancient of Days,
Pavilioned in splendor and girded with praise.
O tell of his might; O sing of his grace,
Whose robe is the light, whose canopy space;
His chariots of wrath the deep thunder clouds form,
And dark is his path on the wings of the storm.

Robert H. Grant, "O Worship the King"

God, Grant Me Serenity

God grant me the serenity to accept the things I cannot change, the courage to change the things I can, and the wisdom to know the difference.

Reinhold Niebuhr

Reinhold Niebuhr, a twentieth-century American theologian, prayed this prayer, which is now quoted in one form or another throughout the world. This request for God's blessings has been a life-changing inspiration to millions of believers.

How we need serenity, courage, and wisdom in our lives! Our days will be transformed when we learn to slow down and distinguish between those godly virtues. If we can make these distinctions, moment by moment, then nothing in the world will disturb our peace.

Only when we realize that God is at work in our lives will we begin to relax and let things happen in due season. Fruit will not ripen any faster because we demand it but will ripen in all its sweet splendor when it is ready, in spite of our demands.

Praying for Others

O Divine Master, grant that I may not so much seek
to be consoled as to console,
to be understood as to understand,
to be loved as to love.

St. Francis of Assisi

Spreading the Word

Father, I thank you for having heard me. I knew that you always hear me, but I have said this for the sake of the crowd standing here, so that they may believe that you sent me.

John 11:41–42

The good news of Jesus is the greatest story ever told, and it cries out to be told again and again in the way Jesus lives through us.

Jesus wanted the crowd to understand that God had sent him. That's why he publicly raised Lazarus from the dead, performing a miracle with God's mighty power working through him. When we witness the wonderful works of our heavenly Father, it is only natural to want to show those wonders to others. In Jesus' case, he was validating his unique role as the Savior of humankind.

As Christians, we walk a fine line between wanting to share our love of God with others and not wanting to overwhelm them with our spirituality. Being a good witness means letting our joy-filled lives stand as the best proof of what God's love can do. Just as Jesus did when he raised Lazarus from the dead, it is best to show, not tell.

When we walk in the light and let God work through us, we will attract others to us, for they will want to know what we know and have what we have. Then we will best be able to tell them the good news about Jesus as the Savior.

Experience It for Yourself

 witness testifies about what he or she has experienced. In order to testify about the living Jesus, you need to know the living Jesus. Keep in touch with Christ, and let him continue to transform your life.

The Prayer of St. Francis

Lord, make me an instrument of Your peace:
where there is hatred, let me show love;
where there is injury, pardon;
where there is doubt, faith;
where there is despair, hope;
and where there is sadness, joy.

O Divine Master, grant that I may not so much seek
to be consoled as to console,
to be understood as to understand,
to be loved as to love.

For it is in giving that we receive,
it is in pardoning that we are pardoned,
and it is in dying that we are born to eternal life.

St. Francis of Assisi

The "Peace Prayer of St. Francis" is one of the most famous and repeated prayers in the world. In praying that he be a vessel through which God's love might touch others as the Lord had done, Francis prayed a classic prayer for the spiritual welfare of others.

Francis of Assisi (1182–1226) was born rich, but he voluntarily became poor and gave his life to the sick and poverty-stricken in his world. Not many of us take Jesus' words literally about forsaking all earthly possessions for his kingdom, but Francis of Assisi took them at face value. For example, as a young man, Francis was once hauled before the local bishop. It seems his father had demanded that Francis return all that he owed his father. In response, Francis stripped himself naked and sent home

Do not worry about anything, but in everything by prayer and supplication with thanksgiving let your requests be made known to God. And the peace of God, which surpasses all understanding, will guard your hearts and your minds in Christ Jesus.

Philippians 4:6–7

the clothes off his back! He then took beggar's clothes and subsequently spent many years ministering among lepers.

In our war-torn world, made even more dangerous by global terrorism, what finer prayer could there be to utter than this one? Nevertheless, the author of this prayer is uncertain. Some scholars date it from the early part of the twentieth century. They point to the fact that it was found in Normandy in 1915, written on the back of a holy card of St. Francis, from which the name comes. Other histories ascribe it to a time before St. Francis, and some believe he did indeed write it.

In any case, all agree that the words of this prayer are an eloquent statement for peace. To give back only good for evil, to always retreat in the face of brutality, to offer peace and love in the face of cruelty—these are the values which, if taken into each individual's heart, would transform the world.

Despite Francis's remarkable compassion for

others, some view Francis as somewhat odd. For example, he even preached to the animals! Yet, one commentator said of him, "Since the nineteenth century, Roman Catholics and Protestants have increasingly seen spiritual sanity in his worldly irrationality. . . . Francis is frequently referred to as either the peculiar saint among the rosebushes or as the conscience of Western civilization, or both."

There is no doubt that Francis can speak to our consciences today. Will you listen? "While you are proclaiming peace with your lips," said Francis, "be careful to have it even more fully in your heart."

God, make me an open vessel through which the waters of your Spirit flow freely. Let your love move through me and out into my world, touching everyone with whom I come in contact. Express your joy through the special talents you have given me, that others may come to know your presence in their own lives by witnessing your presence in mine. Amen.

Muller's Life of Prayer

Dear Father, we thank thee for what thou art going to give us to eat.

George Muller

This prayer is rather unusual. Although George Muller thanked God for his provision, he had no food to feed the children in his orphanage in Bristol, England. Within minutes, however, a baker knocked on the door and brought fresh bread he had made the night before when he could not sleep. Almost immediately, the driver of a milk wagon stopped in front of the orphanage because his wagon had broken down, and he came to the door, wanting to get rid of all his milk so he could get his wagon repaired.

This prayer was characteristic of "Daddy Muller," a man who became a father to the fatherless and cared for over 10,000 children. In 1830, as a young pastor, he determined to depend on God alone to supply his needs—and never again to approach people about them.

Over the next 68 years, he started three orphanages and obtained over seven million dollars through prayer alone. His own salary was about $12,000 a year, most of which he gave away. Muller read the Bible through over 200 times, and he prayed constantly. At the end of his life, he said he had over 50,000 specific answers to his prayers.

Muller was an unusual man with an unusual gift for prayer. The key to his prayer was specificity—praying for the needs of others.

I live in the spirit of prayer. I pray as I walk about, when I lie down and when I rise up. And the answers are always coming. Thousands and tens of thousands of times have my prayers been answered. When once I am persuaded that a thing is right and for the glory of God, I go on praying for it until the answer comes.

George Muller

All You Can

Do all the good you can
By all the means you can,
In all the ways you can,
In all the places you can,
At all the times you can,
To all the people you can,
As long as ever you can.

John Wesley

For we are what he has made us, created in Christ Jesus for good works, which God prepared beforehand to be our way of life.

Ephesians 2:10

This exhortation from the man who founded the Methodist church is, in a way, a prayer for believers to extend God's grace to others through good deeds. Moreover, we should pray not only for the strength and commitment to do good but also for the spiritual and physical welfare of those in need.

Wesley's own faith and works resulted in the founding of hospitals, orphanages, and schools. He also fought for prison reform and the abolition of slavery in eighteenth-century England. Yet, all that he did in his service for the Lord he did on the foundation of his prayers for others.

Prayer and Action

The things, good Lord, that we pray for, give us the grace to labour for.

St. Thomas More

We can easily ask that God's will be done without genuinely caring whether our request is honored. Yet, God finds ways to arouse our interest until we become thoroughly involved. Our prayers mean the most when we're demonstrating their importance by our actions.

Most would agree with the apostle James that faith without corresponding action has little value. Have you found it to be true in your own life? And what in your faith is motivating you to help your neighbor at this moment? Hopefully, you have already prayed for him or her and are now ready to reach out with a loving, helping hand!

What good is it, my brothers and sisters, if you say you have faith but do not have works?

James 2:14

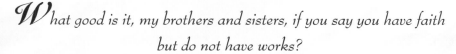

Christ's Own Prayer

*J*esus looked up to heaven and said . . . "Holy Father, protect them in your name that you have given me, so that they may be one, as we are one. While I was with them, I protected them in your name that you have given me. I guarded them, and not one of them was lost except the one destined to be lost, so that the scripture might be fulfilled. But now I am coming to you, and I speak these things in the world so that they may have my joy made complete in themselves. I have given them your word, and the world has hated them because they do not belong to the world, just as I do not belong to the world. I am not asking you to take them out of the world, but I ask you to protect them

*W*eeping may linger for the night, but joy comes with the morning.

Psalm 30:5

from the evil one. They do not belong to the world, just as I do not belong to the world. Sanctify them in the truth; your word is truth. As you have sent me into the world, so I have sent them into the world. And for their sakes I sanctify myself, so that they also may be sanctified in truth.

I ask not only on behalf of these, but also on behalf of those who will believe in me through their word, that they may all be one. As you, Father, are in me and I am in you, may they also be in us, so that the world may believe that you have sent me."

John 17:1, 11–21

This wonderful, comforting passage of Scripture is often called the real

Lord's prayer. The traditional prayer—the one we recite in church—is one Christ prayed when the disciples asked him to teach them to pray. It is a powerful model of how we should pray and what we should pray for. This is Christ's own prayer, however, offered the night he was betrayed. It is an intimate, personal prayer, one which shows his love for his disciples, as well as for us.

Basically, Jesus asked his Father to protect his disciples and to protect those who will believe in him through the testimony of his disciples—in other words, us. Yet, while it is important enough that we are protected, the prayer is more

important for what it says about Jesus' heart. On the eve of his
own death, he was thinking of us, and he wanted us to have
three things.

First, Jesus wanted us to have unity. He prayed,
"Protect them . . . so that they may be one, as we are one."
Throughout his life Jesus had a deep and powerful unity with
his heavenly Father, and he wanted us to have that unity with
each other and with himself. "As you, Father, are in me and
I am in you," he prayed, "may they also be in us, so that the
world may believe that you have sent me."

*His is a loving,
tender hand, full of
sympathy and
compassion.*

Dwight L. Moody

The second thing Jesus wanted us to have was truth and purpose. The unity that he desires for us is based on a common message and a common mission. He has given us the Father's words, and now he sends us out to share those words with others. They are words of truth, he says, words that sanctify us, setting us apart for noble work.

What Jesus seemed to want the most was for us to have his joy. In fact, he says that's why he prayed this prayer "in the earth," while he was still with his disciples. His was an uncommon joy, one he had in his darkest hour. He was one with the Father and obedient to the Father's word, and so his joy was, he says, "complete." This third thing Jesus wanted for us we can have only when we treasure our oneness and his Word.

That was a strange night for the disciples, filled with strange events and strange emotions. Jesus washed their feet and transformed the ancient Passover feast into the Eucharist, or the Lord's Supper. The room was filled with tension, and the danger was great, but then Jesus prayed this tender, gracious prayer, and they were comforted.

Two thousand years later, so are we.

Once God has touched us in the midst of our struggles and has created in us the burning desire to be united forever with him, we will find the courage and the confidence to prepare his way and to invite all who share our life to wait with us during this short time for the day of complete joy. With this new courage and new confidence we can strengthen each other with hopeful words.

Henri J.M. Nouwen, *Reaching Out*

Paul's Encouragement

And this is my prayer, that your love may overflow more and more with knowledge and full insight to help you to determine what is best, so that in the day of Christ you may be pure and blameless, having produced the harvest of righteousness that comes through Jesus Christ for the glory and praise of God.

Philippians 1:9–11

In Paul's letter to the Philippian church, he offers this prayer of encouragement and hope. His fervent wish was that the Philippians would grow in love and insight into the power and the righteous glory of God, which comes through his beloved Son, Christ Jesus.

Paul was anxious to share with others his own love and passion for the life-changing effect Christ's teachings had on him. He sought to spread love and joy to whomever he met, which is the duty of all Christians. Paul was also eager to encourage other Christians to always live righteously, which his own life exemplified.

Praying for others to find and know God or for others to do the right thing is not always easy. We should never force our faith upon others or criticize or judge them if they are hesitant. Rather, as Paul suggests, we should simply pray for them with love that they

might become open to the love of God. Let them feel our joy naturally. Then they will come to Christ, not because they feel they should but because they want to.

When it comes to individual Christians, the Bible's emphasis is not on preaching the gospel to neighbors and friends but on living in a way that causes others to glorify God and on being ready to talk about your faith when people ask.

Paul's Generosity

For this reason I bow my knees before the Father, from whom every family in heaven and on earth takes its name. I pray that, according to the riches of his glory, he may grant that you may be strengthened in your inner being with power through his Spirit, and that Christ may dwell in your hearts through faith, as you are being rooted and grounded in love. I pray that you may have the power to comprehend, with all the saints, what is the breadth and length and height and depth, and to know the love of Christ that surpasses knowledge, so that you may be filled with all the fullness of God.

Now to him who by the power at work within us is able to accomplish abundantly far more than all we can ask or imagine, to him be glory in the church and in Christ Jesus to all generations, forever and ever. Amen.

Ephesians 3:14–21

In Paul's letter to the Ephesians, he wanted very much to share the love of God he had come to know with the believers in this church. This prayer of generosity toward others was typical of Paul, who constantly prayed for the spiritual welfare of others. He hoped that his prayer would help the Christians in Ephesus become "rooted and grounded" in the love of Christ, knowing that this kind of foundation was the bedrock of true happiness and joy.

Make people rejoice in meeting you, feeling that, for them, you are a reason for joy, and that your coming to them is good tidings.

Pope Shenouda III

When we pray for others, we should wish for them the same blessings we wish for ourselves, as Paul had done. Not only will our own hearts soar with unexpected joy, but we will also be passing along encouraging words and thoughts to those who may not yet know the wonder of Christ.

Paul told his readers that the love of Christ "surpasses knowl-

edge" and must be experienced and that he wanted this experience for others. Had Paul not ever experienced this kind of love himself, in no way could he have hoped to "give it away" to others, for you cannot give what you do not have.

Paul was enthused with the fire of a man who knew a secret. His secret was this: God will transform our lives and characters when we let his love flow through us. And we can be a part of that transformation in the lives of others when we let the love of our Lord flow from us to them, particularly in our prayers.

Measure the Spirit's work in your life by your deep abiding joy regardless of life's circumstances.

Wesley L. Duewel, *Measure Your Life*

On Parenting

Father in heaven, give to all parents the resources they require.
Help them to fulfill their promises and keep their hopes.
Strengthen them in difficulty and disappointment.
And make the home of every child a model of your kingdom,
the care of every parent a parable of your love.

Contemporary Prayers for Public Worship

For years, my wife thought that God was angry and impatient with her, always dwelling on her faults. Although we had been raised in the same denomination, I thought God was patient and gentle and always on my side.

This never made sense to us until we realized how different our parents were and how they shaped our understandings of what God was like. It forever changed the way we parent.

Family Faith

I am grateful to God—whom I worship with a clear conscience, as my ancestors did—when I remember you constantly in my prayers night and day. . . . I am reminded of your sincere faith, a faith that lived first in your grandmother Lois and your mother Eunice and now, I am sure, lives in you. For this reason I remind you to rekindle the gift of God that is within you.

2 Timothy 1:3, 5–6

As for me and my household, we will serve the Lord.

Joshua 24:15 NIV

I'm a fifth-generation Floridian, descended, as I like to say, from a long line of horse thieves and bootleggers. The truth is, I was fortunate to have many forebears who honored God. Unlike Timothy, however, I never knew either of my grandmothers, but I did have faithful parents, who made a break with many self-destructive patterns in their own past.

My parents took me to church when I was a youngster, and they did something even more important: They brought their faith home with them. I've seen the worn places on the carpet where my father knelt to pray, and I've listened to my mother often remind me to honor God and serve him. For this reason, I try every day to "rekindle the gift of God that is within me." A heritage of faith is just such a gift—one we pass on to our children and to their children, as Lois did with Timothy.

We are often hindered from giving up our treasures to the Lord out of fear for their safety. This is especially true when those treasures are loved relatives and friends. But we need have no such fears. Our Lord came not to destroy but to save. Everything is safe which we commit to Him, and nothing is really safe which is not so committed.

A.W. Tozer, *The Pursuit of God*

Save Our Children

*Father, hear us, we are praying.
Hear the words our hearts are saying.
We are praying for our children.
Keep them from the powers of evil,
from the secret hidden peril,
from the whirlpool that would suck them,
from the treacherous quicksand, pluck them.
From the worldling's hollow gladness,
from the sting of faithless sadness,
Holy Father, save our children.*

*Through life's troubled waters steer them,
through life's bitter battle cheer them,
Father, Father, be Thou near them.
Read the language of our longing,
read the wordless pleadings thronging,
Holy Father, for our children.
And wherever they may bide,
lead them home at eventide.*

Amy Carmichael, *Toward Jerusalem*

In the fear of the Lord one has strong confidence, and one's children will have a refuge.

Proverbs 14:26

A lot of people pray for children. Amy Carmichael was one of them, but she did more than just pray for them. As a missionary in India, she saw young girls being sold as temple prostitutes, and she decided to do something about it.

She began to buy them herself and to rescue them, even against the opposition of townspeople and authorities. Any girl who escaped from the temple was welcomed at the home and school she established. Before her death in 1951, she had provided a new life for over 1,000 children—a perfect example of what the apostle James taught: that believing and doing go together.

Her life and their lives were changed after she had a vision of Jesus weeping and praying for the children. Such a vision will change us as well, and we can love them in both word and deed—with prayer and action.

~~~

Surrendering to God

Lord, I give up all my own plans and purposes, all my own desires and hopes, and accept Thy will for my life. I give myself, my life, my all utterly to Thee to be Thine forever.

Amy Carmichael

Our Restless Hearts

*Thou hast made us for Thyself,
And our hearts are restless until they rest in Thee.*

St. Augustine

Augustine was the Bishop of Hippo in Africa for part of the fourth and fifth centuries. He was considered the church's foremost thinker for a thousand years between the apostle Paul and the theologian Thomas Aquinas. Yet, he was born a farmer's son in humble circumstances.

As a young man, he wrote the *Confessions*, personal memoirs that narrated his search for earthly satisfaction. His experimentations often resulted in a guilty conscience. His life changed radically, however, when he realized that his spiritual restlessness would continue until he finally gave his heart to a peaceful rest in God.

Augustine's prayer still has great life-changing potential for us today. By declaring our restlessness as a normal part of our creaturehood, it points us to a greater reality. There is more to existence than what we see and touch. We can let our anxieties push us to find it, to question our true purposes in life, and to surrender to God. We can let our daily agitation call us to more meaningful priorities. In other words, we, too, can arrive at a rest in God as the Satisfier of our souls.

Later in life, Augustine penned *The City of God,* which laid out a vision of God's will and ways in human society. He wrote it during a time when his own home in North Africa stood on the brink of terrorist attack. Thus, in his day and ours, this truth remains: God is the ultimate source of our security.

Lord, grant me a simple, kind, open, believing, loving and generous heart, worthy of being your dwelling place.

John Sergieff

Third-Step Prayer

~

God, I offer myself to Thee, to build with me and to do with me as Thou wilt. Relieve me of the bondage of self, that I may better do Thy will. Take away my difficulties, that victory over them may bear witness to those I would help of Thy Power, Thy Love, and Thy Way of life. May I do Thy will always!

From "Alcoholics Anonymous" *The Big Book*

The 12-step program of Alcoholics Anonymous has changed millions of lives. People who were lost, alone, forgotten, and

diseased have been healed and returned to wholeness by this spiritually empowering program that relies on reaching out to God for help.

Known to all 12-steppers is this "Third-Step Prayer," which requires a total surrender to the will of God—for God

to do for us what we could not do for ourselves. Yet, anyone who is struggling can say this prayer and let God change their lives and their behavior.

The idea that we can offer ourselves to God to build a new life is truly wonderful and hopeful. To be relieved of the bondage of destructive habits empowers us to live by God's Spirit, where truth is found. Moreover, to show others our victory over our difficulties is the kind of testimony that draws people closer to God.

Pray this prayer whether you have an addiction or not, whether you are a 12-stepper or not, and you will reap the untold blessings that come from surrendering your life to our heavenly Father.

As we felt new power flow in, as we enjoyed peace of mind, as we discovered we could face life successfully, as we became conscious of His presence, we began to lose our fear of today, tomorrow or the hereafter. We were reborn.

From *The Big Book* of Alcoholics Anonymous

*W*hen "Dr. Bob" and "Bill W." established Alcoholics Anonymous in 1939, they had no idea how their healing program would affect so many lives in the years to follow. The program actually began in 1935 in Akron, Ohio, with a handful of members. The second group appeared in New York in 1937. Today, there are thousands of AA groups in dozens of countries throughout the world, helping millions of hopeful men and women to reclaim their lives.

Even today, over 60 years later, very little about the program or its text, The Big Book, *has changed.* AA has inspired other 12-step programs such as Cocaine Anonymous, Narcotics Anonymous, Over-Eaters Anonymous, and Gamblers Anonymous.

All and Nothing

❧

Let us therefore desire nothing else, wish for nothing else, and let nothing please and delight us except our Creator and Redeemer, and Savior, the only true God, who is full of good, who alone is good, . . . and from whom, and through whom, and in whom is all mercy, all grace, all glory of all penitents and of the just, and of all the blessed rejoicing in heaven.

St. Francis of Assisi

For St. Francis, it's not all *or* nothing. It's all *and* nothing.

Even if we receive and delight only in God's gifts, we end up with all the mercy, grace, glory, and joy heaven has to offer. When we surrender ourselves entirely to the Lord, we will get everything that truly matters. In essence, we give up things that don't last, and we receive things that do.

It's not a bad trade.

❧

Whom have I in heaven but you? And there is nothing on earth that I desire other than you.

Psalm 73:25

Surrendering Our Hearts

*A*lmighty God,
unto whom all hearts are open,
all desires known,
and from whom no secrets are hid:
Cleanse the thoughts of our hearts,
by the inspiration of thy Holy Spirit:
that we may perfectly love thee,
and worthily magnify thy holy name.

Book of Common Prayer

The truly life-changing prayer of surrender is to ask God not only to cleanse us from our sinful deeds but also to purge the thoughts of our hearts. For what we are doing on the outside is surely no larger a concern to God than what we are becoming on the inside.

When we surrender ourselves to God this way, he will
transform our character. Then the world will see the Lord
living in us despite the failures in our lives.

*Help me know that wringing my hands in the wake of failure is as
useless as lamenting storm-felled trees. . . . But what could happen if
I picked up a saw and took to that tree, making wood for a fire
around which friends can gather?*

God's Loving Will

Take, O Lord, and receive my entire liberty, my memory, my understanding and my whole will. All that I am and all that I possess You have given me. I surrender it all to You to be disposed of according to Your will. Give me only Your love and Your grace; with these I will be rich enough, and will desire nothing more.

St. Ignatius Loyola

While Inigo de Loyola was recuperating from a severe leg injury, he underwent a life-changing experience. For several weeks, he had been cloistered in a castle, where out of sheer boredom he picked up a book on the life of Christ and Christian saints. As he read, he felt a strong connection with the saints and their lives of devotion to Christ.

"Ignatius," as he would become known, eventually met with the Pope, traveled to the Holy Land on pilgrimage, and studied Latin in Barcelona, where he became a priest. So zealous was he in his desire to teach others how to pray, the Inquisition jailed him for 42 days.

Nothing prevented Ignatius from becoming a successful spiritual writer, teacher, and beloved Jesuit priest and from establishing Jesuit schools and universities all over the world. Ignatius was beatified on July 27, 1609, and canonized in 1622. To this day, Christians who seek to express their love for the Lord reverently recite his prayers.

This particular prayer is a prayer of surrender—of completely giving oneself over to God and his will and of asking

The glory of God is a person fully alive.

Irenaeus

only for his love and grace in return. How Ignatius must have felt, loving a God so strongly and being so strongly loved in return! Yet, this same love is available to all of us should we desire it.

Worth more than all the gold and silver and monetary riches in the world, God's loving will for our lives is one of the most precious gifts we are ever given. To recognize, as Ignatius did, that all that we are is because of God and that all we have been given comes from God is a wisdom the soul longs to know and understand. To give ourselves over to this wisdom and let it guide our lives is to be who God intended us to be.

Jesus has told us that we should desire only the kingdom of

God and that all else would be given to us once we entered his kingdom. Ignatius tells us that once we receive the glory of God's loving grace, we will desire nothing more, for we will have everything.

Ignatius founded the Society of Jesus, and their motto was *Ad Majorem Dei Gloriam.* It means "to the greater glory of God." Everything he did was for the love of God, and that was the secret to his success, his achievements, and his joy. What a lesson he has left for us—to discover just how fulfilling our lives can be if we do everything for the greater glory of God.

God uses unexpected vessels to show us that he is the one who is really performing the miracle. It is not necessary to attend a healing crusade featuring a prominent personality to experience a miracle, although there are certainly times when God uses such means as well. Just as often, he will choose to use someone of modest stature, who has the heart of a servant.

A Bargain With God

"With what shall I come before the Lord, and bow myself before God on high? Shall I come before him with burnt offerings, with calves a year old? Will the Lord be pleased with thousands of rams, with ten thousands of rivers of oil? Shall I give my firstborn for my transgression, the fruit of my body for the sin of my soul?" He has told you, O mortal, what is good; and what does the Lord require of you but to do justice, and to love kindness, and to walk humbly with your God?

Micah 6:6–8

Micah of Moresheth tells us that God requires only that we be just, kind, and humble. Yet, how often do we think that we must offer "bargaining chips" in order to get our prayers answered and make God smile

down upon us? How often do we barter with God to get what we want when all God wants is for us to walk in his ways?

What God requires is not burnt offerings—calves, rams, or rivers of oil. God cares not for material goods. After all, he made them! What God requires of us is simply what Jesus taught his disciples: Love God with all your heart, soul, and mind, and love your neighbor as yourself. That's all it takes.

The quality of mercy is not strained.
It droppeth as the gentle rain from heaven
Upon the place beneath: it is twice blessed:
It blesseth him that gives and him that takes.

William Shakespeare, *The Merchant of Venice*

Opening Up to God

I give this time to You alone. Please guide me in this prayer. I ask only for honesty and total sincerity. May I pray from my heart alone. If there is anything I should experience now, or any words I should hear, I am ready to receive them. In stillness and quiet listening, I now open myself to You.

Hugh Prather, *The Quiet Answer*

When we open a gift or a letter, we look forward to bringing into view what has been hidden. This is usually a matter of happy anticipation since we hope to have a sense of joy in what others have sent to us.

In the same way, we can open ourselves to God, as Prather's prayer shows us. This surrendering to our Creator will change us if we let it. Yet, it's not as easy as opening a package, because we may have learned through painful experience that if we open ourselves to another, we may not receive the care and respect we deeply wanted. This unspoken fear in our hearts may also keep us closed to all that the Lord wants us to experience and hear.

The special, life-changing movement in our lives is this: coming to know our God as so good and gentle that we will have no hesitation to open our hearts to him. Thus, when he invites, we will respond. When he calls, we will listen. When he knocks, we will open our whole heart.

When our will is surrendered to God . . . then disappointment becomes His appointment, and life is no longer a ceaseless struggle to get Him to do something that we think He ought to do.

Alan Redpath, *Victorious Christian Living*

Comfort Foods

As a deer longs for flowing streams, so my soul longs for you, O God. My soul thirsts for God, for the living God. When shall I come and behold the face of God? My tears have been my food day and night, while people say to me continually, "Where is your God?"

These things I remember, as I pour out my soul: how I went with the throng, and led them in procession to the house of God, with glad shouts and songs of thanksgiving, a multitude keeping festival. Why are you cast down, O my soul, and why are you disquieted within me? Hope in God; for I shall again praise him, my help and my God.

Psalm 42:1–6

Think of a food or drink you love, not because you need it, but because the taste of it brings you joy. All of us have such foods. We call them comfort foods—foods that remind us of home and make us feel secure.

I take comfort in a number of Southern foods, including ice tea (sweetened, of course) and even grits, especially served with fish, like the grits my grandfather used to serve for breakfast. Often our comfort foods and drinks are not fancy or expensive. They just evoke powerful memories and relationships, creating a thirst or appetite for the familiar and for the sacred.

For each of us, there is some great longing for which there are few satisfactions. In the same way a deer bounding through the forest pants for a drink from a cool, fresh spring, we all long for something satisfying, and in this prayer we are

The Lord will guide you always; he will satisfy your needs in a sun-scorched land and will strengthen your frame. You will be like a well-watered garden, like a spring whose waters never fail.

Isaiah 58:11 NIV

reminded that this longing is a picture of our soul's own great need for God.

It is a powerful image. I know of at least four musical settings for this psalm, one of which is what I call a road song—a song I sing late at night when I'm driving and everyone else is asleep. For me, it speaks to a deep and mysterious longing for God, a recognition of what several writers have referred to as a God-shaped vacuum in our hearts. I can barely sing it without weeping.

This longing is palatable and insatiable. The closer we get to God, the thirstier for him we become. According to St. Bernard of Clairvaux, we first taste the sweetness of God in our prayers, and then "Once the sweetness of God has been tasted, it draws us to the pure love of God

more than our needs compel us to love him." In other words, we eventually want God more than we want the things God gives us. In one of his hymns, Bernard wrote:

> We taste Thee, O Thou Living Bread,
> And long to feast upon Thee still:
> We drink of Thee, the Fountainhead
> And thirst our souls from Thee to fill.

It is this craving that leads the psalmist to "the house of God, with glad shouts and songs of thanksgiving." And it is this craving that prayer creates as it changes our deepest desire.

*A*ll my life long I had panted
For a drink from some cool spring
That I hoped would quench the burning
Of the thirst I felt within.
Feeding on the husks around me,
Till my strength was gone:
Longed my soul for something better,
Only still to hunger on.
Well of water, ever springing,
Bread of life, so rich and free,
Untold wealth that never faileth
My redeemer is to me.
Hallelujah! I have found Him
Whom my soul so long hath craved!
Jesus satisfies my longings;
Through his blood I now am saved.

Teresa's Quest

I am yours, you made me.
I am yours, you called me.
I am yours, you saved me.
I am yours, you loved me.
I will never leave your presence.

Teresa of Avila

Have you ever wished you could be entirely at one with God? If so, your heart beats in tandem with Teresa's. She was a famous Spanish mystic who sought perfect union with the Lord. She even spoke of her relationship with him as a "mystical marriage."

Teresa's quest, however, wasn't a solitary pursuit, something that would take place in private and move her to desert places so she could be alone. Instead, Teresa's love for God caused her to start 17 religious houses, where she would serve others while writing about her experiences with God.

What a deep sense of God's presence!

The upright shall live in your presence.

Psalm 140:13

Always Faithful

The thought of my affliction and my homelessness is wormwood and gall! My soul continually thinks of it and is bowed down within me. But this I call to mind, and therefore I have hope: The steadfast love of the Lord never ceases, his mercies never come to an end; they are new every morning; great is your faithfulness. "The Lord is my portion," says my soul, "therefore I will hope in him."

Lamentations 3:19–24

How often do we cave in to negativity and despair? How often does the appearance of lack cause us to give in to doubt? How often do we cry out because we are suffering? How often do we dwell on a fearful situation, letting it sap our strength and weigh down our spirit?

The message of this prayer by Jeremiah, who suffered because he stood up for God against God's enemies, is that no matter how low we feel, if we surrender to God, he will lift us up to a place where we can gain new perspective and experience new mercies. The love of the Lord gives us hope because it never ceases, even if our circumstances give us the impression that God has left us stranded. In other words, God is always faithful to us, even if we lose faith in him.

What this prayer tells us is that thoughts have the power to affect our lives. Change your thoughts, and change your life. Think not of wormwood and gall but rather of the Lord's never-ending mercies. Surrender to God's love and goodness.

In the depth of my pain, I cry out to God. In grief and sorrow, in loss and anguish, I cry out to God. When I am overwhelmed and cannot bear another moment, I cry out to God. And he hears my cry. He listens and cares and answers, as he has throughout all time.

Picturing the Lord

~~~

My dearest Lord,
Be thou a bright flame before me,
Be thou a guiding star above me,
Be thou a smooth path beneath me,
Be thou a kindly shepherd behind me,
Today and for evermore.

Saint Colomba

With the dawning of each new day, we need courage to take each new step in the walk of faith. Thankfully, we have God's bright guidance, his smooth pathways, and his gentle leadership.

Colomba must have known these things well. He was an Irish missionary who lived from 521 to 597. He journeyed to share the love of God with villagers who lived off the coast of Scotland on the island of Iona. Colomba's preaching even warmed the heart of the king of the Picts, who joined the young man's church.

In this prayer Colomba depicted the Lord under four images—as a fire, a star, a path, and a shepherd. What modern pictures or similes would you use for your own relationship with the Lord? For most of us, even in our thoroughly modern situations, the image of a shepherd still speaks of the things we most need and want in our daily lives. For so often we feel like vulnerable sheep walking along paths that can be rocky and dangerous.

Yet, as Colomba affirms, if we stumble or lose our way, like a shepherd of infinite good will, our Shepherd picks us up and puts us back on the path. Therefore, let us be assured: *Even if we lose faith for a while, he will never lose us.*

Trust in the Lord with all your heart, and do not rely on your own insight. In all your ways acknowledge him, and he will make straight your paths.

Proverbs 3:5–6

A Holy Heart

Lord, grant me a holy heart
that sees always what is fine and pure
and is not frightened at the sight of sin
but creates order wherever it goes.
Grant me a heart that knows nothing of boredom,
Weeping and sighing.

Let me not be too concerned
with the bothersome thing I call "myself."
Lord, give me a sense of humor
And I will find happiness in life and profit for others.

St. Thomas More

Convictions were costly in the days of Thomas More (1478–1535). Remaining true to his Christian heritage, he refused support for the edicts of Henry VIII, king of England, because they were contrary to the teachings of Christ. Thus, More was eventually placed in the Tower of London, accused of treason, and beheaded.

His prayer for a holy heart might well have been written during his stay in prison while he patiently awaited his death. Any of us who feel imprisoned by a current crisis or a physical malady can pray these words along with More—that we not be frightened, not succumb to apathy, and not be overwhelmed with weeping and sighing. Instead, we should surrender ourselves totally to the God who loves us.

In every waking moment, Lord, it seems my heart stretches for this one thing: your love.

Our discouraged spirit will once again know joy when we realize that there is a deeper reality to our lives, a level of truth only the heart can understand. That truth is this: There is a wonderful master plan at work in our lives, and the one who guides our path loves us more than we can ever imagine.

It is a great compliment to More's character that, while he was surely experiencing the worst anxiety, he nevertheless prayed to be less concerned with himself—a "bothersome thing." In this regard, note the unselfish sentiments that fill his final letter, written to his daughter Margaret with a charcoal stick on July 5, 1535, the day before he was executed: "Our Lord bless you, good daughter, and your good husband, and your little boy, and all yours, and all my children, and all my god-children and all our friends. . . . I cumber you, good Margaret, much, but I would be sorry if it should be any longer

than to-morrow. . . and therefore, to-morrow long I to go to God. It were a day very meet and convenient for me."

More's surrender to God was complete in every way.

The God who hung the stars in space will turn
Your darkness into light.
The God whose birds rise on the winds will give
Your injured soul new flight.
The God who taught the whale its song will cause
Your heart to sing again.
For the God whose power made earth and sky will touch
You with his gentle hand.

The Devotion of St. Francis

M̄ay the power of your love, O Lord, fiery and sweet as honey, wean my heart from all that is under heaven, so that I may die for love of your love, you who were so good as to die for love of my love.

St. Francis of Assisi

Giovanni Francesco di Pietro di Bernardone, the much-beloved St. Francis of Assisi, was born into a wealthy family before hearing God's call as a young man to rebuild a local church. Then, in 1209, he sensed a life-long calling to imitate Christ by living a life of chastity, obedience, and poverty.

Francis abandoned his family wealth and lived a life of personal poverty. After he made his vow, he borrowed a scarecrow's rope-belt to encircle the robe he would wear for the rest of his life. Though considered a great mystic, he was practical, too; he started a ministry for the sick and directed it until he died.

We can feel the passion of his devotion exuding from this prayer. He asked God to wean his heart from everything on earth that might tempt him to love the love of God any less. If he were with us today, he would invite all of us to do the same. Such a life-changing act of trust and dependence for Francis was the very purpose of his life.

We are often hindered from giving up our treasures to the Lord out of fear for their safety . . . . But we need have no such fears. Our Lord came not to destroy but to save. Everything is safe which we commit to Him.

A. W. Tozer, *The Pursuit of God*

Shine Through Me

To pray for holiness is to pray for wholeness, in body, mind, and spirit. And there is no better way to become whole than to allow ourselves to become one with Jesus Christ.

Dear Jesus, help me to spread your fragrance everywhere. Flood my soul with your spirit and life. Penetrate and possess my whole being so utterly that all my life may be only a radiance of yours. Shine through me and be so in me that every person I come in contact with may feel your Presence in my soul. Let them look up and see no longer me but only Jesus.

John Henry Newman

For Roman Catholic cardinal John Henry Newman, spreading the holy fragrance of Christ was more than a heart's desire, it was his vocation and calling. In this poetic prayer full of potent imagery, he speaks of the "Presence" of Christ as a force that shines so brightly and so completely that it possesses his being to the point of reflecting his union with the Lord.

Our lives are truly transformed when we seek to fill ourselves with the Holy Spirit, allowing it to penetrate our being and radiate outward to touch those we come in contact with. No longer are we merely human beings but spiritual beings having a human experience. No longer are we just a man or woman but an image of Jesus himself.

Lord, make me whole.
Like the woman who touched your cloak for healing,
I reach out to you, O Lord.
Hoping, believing, trusting, longing for your power.
I don't want to be some otherworldly pious person.
I don't need other people to say, "There goes someone holy!"
I just want to please you with my life.
Fill me with your fullness.
Make me all you created me to be.

David's Lament

Here I pause in my sojourning,
giving thanks for having come,
come to trust, at every turning,
God will guide me safely home.
Jesus sought me when a stranger,
wandering from the fold of God,
Came to rescue me from danger,
precious presence, precious blood.

Robert Robinson,
"Come, Thou Fount, of Every Blessing"

I am a worm, and not human; scorned by others, and despised by the people. All who see me mock at me; they make mouths at me, they shake their heads; "Commit your cause to the Lord; let him deliver—let him rescue the one in whom he delights!"

Yet it was you who took me from the womb; you kept me safe on my mother's breast. On you I was cast from my birth, and since my mother bore me you have

been my God. Do not be far from me, for trouble is near and there is no one to help.

Psalm 22:6–11

David is the author of this prayer, which mentions how people often ridiculed him mercilessly, particularly when he was young. His brothers laughed at him when he said he would kill the giant Goliath, and even the giant mocked him before they battled. Nevertheless, David was confident that God would deliver him. In fact, David held this assurance in the Lord throughout his life, even when he fled from his palace because his own son, Absalom, tried to usurp the throne. Yet, in each case, the Lord stood with him, and David overcame his enemies.

Most of us will never fight a giant or a bear, at least not the kind with arms and legs, but we will encounter immense

problems, and some people will expect us to fail. That's when the words of this prayer should echo our surrender to the Lord: "Commit your cause to the Lord; let him deliver—let him rescue the one in whom he delights!"

David said to Saul, "Your servant has been keeping his father's sheep. When a lion or a bear came and carried off a sheep from the flock, I went after it, struck it and rescued the sheep from its mouth. When it turned on me, I seized it by its hair, struck it and killed it. Your servant has killed both the lion and the bear; this uncircumcised Philistine will be like one of them, because he has defied the armies of the living God. The Lord who delivered me from the paw of the lion and the paw of the bear will deliver me from the hand of this Philistine." Saul said to David, "Go, and the Lord be with you."

1 Samuel 17:34–37 NIV

All Things From Thy Goodness

O Heart of Love, I place all my trust in Thee, for I fear all things from my own weakness, but I hope for all things from Thy goodness.

St. Margaret Mary

Be led, pay attention to God's voice, and follow step by step.

After suffering a severe case of rheumatic fever, Margaret Mary Alacoque entered a French convent in 1671 to devote herself to the Sacred Heart of the Lord. She was canonized in 1920, and her feast day is observed on October 17.

In this prayer, she surrenders her trust to the Lord, fearing that her own weakness might be keeping her from doing God's will. We, too, often fear that our way of doing things will fail and only make things worse. By surrendering to God and placing our faith and trust in him alone, we, too, can hope for and receive, "all things from Thy goodness."

Fulfill My Heart's Desire

Searcher of spirits,
Try Thou my reins and heart,
Cleanse Thou my inward part,
Turn, overturn, and turn.
Wood, hay and stubble see,
Spread out before Thee,
Burn, burn.

Savior of sinners,
Out of the depths I cry,
Perfect me or I die:
Perfect me, patient One;
In thy revealing light,
I stand confused outright,
Undone.

O to be holy!
Thou wilt not say me nay

Who movest me to pray.
Enable to endure:
Spiritual cleansing Fire,
Fulfill my heart's desire,
Make pure.

Amy Carmichael, *God's Missionary*

The famous missionary Amy Carmichael was not always as submissive to God as this prayer implies. She described herself as a "wild Irish girl" who argued with God about the color of her eyes—she wanted blue instead of brown. She also argued with him about being single and celibate when she wanted a husband.

As a young missionary in Japan and later China, she was often sick. More notably, she resisted the rules of her mission and was generally troublesome. Yet, when she arrived in India, her life changed. We can assume her prayers changed as well. She lived in India for 55 years, where she founded a school and a home for children.

Her spirit changed as did the requests of her prayers, which ultimately became "Fulfill my heart's desire, make pure."

Consecrate yourselves therefore, and be holy; for I am the Lord your God.

Leviticus 20:7

Both Big and Small

Here I am, Lord, body, heart and soul.
Grant that with your love,
I may be big enough to reach the world,
And small enough to be at one with you.

Mother Teresa

Many of us, when we approach the spiritual life, see only two options: We either give ourselves to social service to help those in need, or we move inward in a life-long pursuit of fellowship with God.

Mother Teresa was able to combine both of these legitimate callings of the Spirit. Her prayer declares her desire to be both big and small. To be big in acts of human kindness and to be small enough to know the great God as fully as possible.

Both approaches to religion can change our lives forever. Let us attempt them, and let us take Mother Teresa's example to heart. She was best known for her selfless acts of compassion. Yet, she had the time and energy to maintain a

vibrant spiritual life, writing numerous prayers and devotionals for her fellow workers.

Perhaps Teresa's greatest lesson to us is this: It is always best to keep big and small together. That way, we can give our best to both the Creator and humanity.

Let go and let God see you through.
Give in and let God be with you.
Surrender to a love that heals all things.
Let go and let God be your wings.

Here I Am

And all of us, with unveiled faces, seeing the glory of the Lord as though reflected in a mirror, are being transformed into the same image from one degree of glory to another; for this comes from the Lord, the Spirit.

2 Corinthians 3:18

*My God,
here I am,
my heart devoted to you.
Fashion me
according to your heart.*

Brother Lawrence

His birth name was Nicolas Herman, but he became known to history as Brother Lawrence, a monk who lived in the seventeenth century. We might think of him as a religious chef, for he spent much of his time in the kitchen, either cooking or scrubbing pots and pans. His set of spiritual maxims have urged believers in Christ to "practice the presence of God," no matter where they may be.

The beauty of this direct approach to God is that it makes the divine-human relationship quite real and available. Even if we're washing the dishes or mowing the lawn, our hearts can be centered in God.

Topical Index